WHEN THE
PRESSURE'S
ON

WHEN THE PRESSURE'S ON

LOUIS S. CSOKA

THE SECRET TO WINNING WHEN YOU CAN'T AFFORD TO LOSE

AMACOM

AMERICAN MANAGEMENT ASSOCIATION

New York • Atlanta • Brussels • Chicago • Mexico City • San Francisco
Shanghai • Tokyo • Toronto • Washington, D.C.

www.amacombooks.org/go/specialsales
Or contact special sales:
Phone: 800-250-5308
Email: specialsls@amanet.org
View all the AMACOM titles at: www.amacombooks.org
American Management Association: www.amanet.org

Library of Congress Cataloging-in-Publication Data

Names: Csoka, Louis Stephen, 1941- author.
Title: When the pressure's on : the secret to winning when you can't afford to lose / by Louis S. Csoka.
Description: New York : American Management Association, 2016. | Includes index.
Identifiers: LCCN 2015050001 (print) | LCCN 2016001157 (ebook) | ISBN 9780814436103 (hardcover) | ISBN 9780814436110 (ebook)
Subjects: LCSH: Success in business. | Performance–Psychological aspects. | Goal setting in personnel management. | Stress management. | Leadership.
Classification: LCC HF5386 .C8986 2016 (print) | LCC HF5386 (ebook) | DDC 658.4/09–dc23

About AMA
American Management Association (www.amanet.org) is a world leader in talent development, advancing the skills of individuals to drive business success. Our mission is to support the goals of individuals and organizations through a complete range of products and services, including classroom and virtual seminars, webcasts, webinars, podcasts, conferences, corporate and government solutions, business books, and research. AMA's approach to improving performance combines experiential learning—learning through doing—with opportunities for ongoing professional growth at every step of one's career journey.

To my patient wife, Judy and my children Christa, Tracy, Nancy, and Matt who supported and encouraged me all these years to follow my dreams and to write my dang book! To all my family and friends (impossible to list them all), I wouldn't be the person I am or be where I am today without your continuous love and support.

CONTENTS

9

10

FOREWORD

by ROBERT BROOKS BROWN,
LIEUTENANT GENERAL, U.S. ARMY

DESERT STORM HAD JUST been won in a resounding victory, and fresh from the ticker tape parade in New York City was the man who led the United States to victory, General Norman Schwarzkopf. In 1992, he visited his alma mater, the United States Military Academy at West Point. One of his key stops was a new and innovative center that was working on improving human performance. In a scene I will never forget, General Schwarzkopf sat in an egg-shaped chair hooked up to biofeedback equipment. He was asked to think about a situation that made him mad—the biofeedback readings were nearly off the computer screen. Then he was asked to think about a situation that would relax him and the readings dropped to a very low level. General Schwarzkopf clearly understood how critical it is to maintain control in life or death situations; he referred to an example of combat in Vietnam when he was a younger officer and his unit was caught in an ambush. He remembered experiencing a calm, almost like things were moving in slow motion in the middle of the chaos as he gave directions to soldiers and they gained the upper hand on the enemy. He was clearly in "the zone" during this life-or-death situation. He had not experienced that type of slow motion control since he was on the football field years earlier at West Point.

Coaches, surgeons, military leaders, business leaders, and numerous successful leaders from all different fields have visited the Center for Enhanced Performance at West Point and all completely understood the efforts to develop leaders with effective mental tools to deal with the challenges ahead. I was a young captain with about ten years in the Army when I had the privilege of working alongside the brainchild of this innovative center, Colonel (Dr.) Louis Csoka. A West Point graduate who led troops in combat in Vietnam and a brilliant professor in the Behavioral Sciences and Leadership Department at West Point for many years, Dr. Csoka would go on to develop revolutionary techniques for leaders to excel in any given field. His efforts would lead to critical changes in leadership development with an emphasis not only on physical development, but on gaining the mental skills needed for success.

One of his key strategies was to properly develop effective goal-setting skills. Tough, demanding, yet realistic and measurable goals are key to enhancing performance in any field. Teaching West Point cadets these goal-setting skills led to increased performance in the classroom, on the athletic fields, and in their leadership abilities as future Army lieutenants. I continued to use these goal-setting skills successfully throughout the next twenty-six years in the Army, working with formations as small as thirty soldiers to as large as 100,000 soldiers. Initially, we relied on instinct to know these skills would work; experts can now prove that goal setting focuses the brain to achieve a task. Dr. Csoka's innovative methods were well ahead of their time and he has truly been an innovator in enhancing mental performance.

Nearly every Army manual on leadership asks leaders to visualize the battlefield and provide clear guidance to their subordinates on how to defeat an enemy force. Dr. Csoka clearly understood that the skill of visualization was critical to success—and that it could be taught. I watched him teach a room full of tough, gritty West Point football players to visualize a situation and mentally practice using scenes from popular Walt Disney movies. He was also among the first in this field to tape a camera to the helmet of a football player so they could see the scout team replicating the opposing team's offense numerous times and learn to visualize more effectively.

Using Csoka's techniques, I worked with a West Point swimmer who was incredibly talented but let his nerves get the best of him prior to competitions. After he learned to visualize his race effectively, he could essentially swim the event mutiple times before it actually took place. He went on to the national championships in swimming and was able to take advantage of his potential. Dr. Csoka's techniques have proven effective throughout the Army as we worked with various Army units, the Army's National Training Center, and elite organizations like the Special

Operations forces and the Army's Golden Knights parachute team.

Soldiers are consistently preparing for the demanding physical challenges of combat operations. Dr. Csoka used research, studies, and his years of experience in this field to determine the mental skills needed for the stress and challenges of life or death situations in combat. He proved that focus and concentration skills could be measured, honed, and improved, and developed the techniques to cultivate the energy management abilities that enable an individual to get calmer in stressful situations. I learned to improve my own skills through Dr. Csoka's effective teaching methods, which clearly show leaders can improve their mental skills and should consistently work as hard on their mental condition as they do the physical. When faced with life or death situations in combat operations, I found that I would get calmer as the situation became more intense. For a leader to be calm in the middle of the storm is certainly an effective tool.

As a pioneer in the field of mental skills and human performance, Dr. Csoka faced numerous challenges throughout his journey to develop effective techniques for leaders in all fields. Naysayers considered the techniques in mental skills training to be guesswork and argued that people either had the skills or they did not. This is where Dr. Csoka revealed his true genius as he would not be deterred by those who just did not understand. He had seen these mental techniques work in the toughest conditions and he revealed an incredible passion to learn more about the brain and prove that leaders can build the mental skills required to excel. Early on in his work the mental skills were referred to as "enhanced performance." Today these skills are considered essential for leaders in all fields who face complexity unlike that in any time in our history. The challenges today are the immense amounts of information available and the incredible speed at which that information rapidly diffuses. Leaders today require Dr. Csoka's mental skills to make effective decisions in a timely manner more than ever before.

In this book you will not only learn techniques to improve your effectiveness as a leader, but you will also be inspired by the vision, persistence, and courage of a true leader in his field—a man who helped set the foundation for effective development of those mental skills required to thrive in a complex world.

INTRODUCTION

REGARDLESS OF THEIR CAREER stats, NFL kickers are only as good as their last kicks. One mistake, one missed field goal, and their careers could be over. To have any chance of sustained success, they must be able to line up for every kick, without letting the fear of missing or getting cut distract them from the task at hand. That is why when Billy Cundiff was released by the Atlanta Falcons in 2007, he knew he needed help.

Billy started his career on a high note; he was signed by the Dallas Cowboys as an undrafted free agent in 2002. After missing two field goals in a critical game in 2005, however, he was released. Then he was signed and released by teams at a surprising pace, playing in four different cities in two years. After being released again in 2007, he asked his coach for advice during his exit interview. The coach told him to work on the mental side of things and referred him to my company, Apex Performance. "It turns out my thought patterns were bringing me down," Billy said. "I had to get to a place where I was confident, without being arrogant."

I worked with Billy on setting goals, stress management,

and mental preparation. "I realized that I was capable of much more than what I had been doing," Billy told me. To achieve peak performance, he needed to center his own thoughts and mental preparedness, and he learned that it did not matter what eighty thousand other people thought, whether they were cheering for him to miss or jeering him because he had. He became mentally strong, able to bear the weight of kicks that could be the difference between victory and defeat. It changed the trajectory of his career.

In 2010, while playing for the Baltimore Ravens, Billy was selected for the Pro Bowl. "For me, going from having to compete for my job to start the season to being voted by my peers as being the top kicker in the AFC was pretty nice."

What I taught Billy comes from both personal and professional experience. As a cadet at the United States Military Academy at West Point and later as a soldier in Vietnam, I learned the importance of mental preparation. Years later, as a professor at West Point, where I conducted research on performance enhancement, I approached our football coach about teaching his players the mental skills he talked about with them: visualization, confidence, poise, and focus. He allowed me to work with several players on the team, and I used sports psychology and the newest science in biofeedback, making my research an evidence-based program. West Point went on to have one of the most successful seasons in years, and from there the program was expanded to all cadets.

Years later as head of human resources at New Holland, a $6 billion agriculture and construction equipment manufacturing company, I adapted this program for the business world. In my day-to-day dealings with the company's management team, I gained insight into the pressures and demands placed on these executives. Their stress levels were off the charts. The company, like so many others, provided no resources to help these managers cope, let alone thrive, in an environment that kept them under fire at all times. I witnessed far too many people under these conditions making bad decisions, exhibiting poor problem-solving skills, and experiencing interpersonal confrontations, all of which were a threat not only to the success of the company but to the overall health and wellness of the company's executives.

I realized the skills I had taught athletes and soldiers could be beneficial for businesspeople as well. I expanded my research and found that the concepts I had developed on peak performance and mental training applied no matter what challenge you faced—even if you are not under actual fire, even if you are not lining up a kick to win the Super Bowl, it can feel that way. After leaving New Holland, I was the executive coach for Fred Rockwood, who was the CEO of Hillenbrand, Inc., at the time. He understood the issues his executives faced and how powerful this type of integrated training could be. In 2002 we implemented the first ever peak performance center in a Fortune 500 company, putting into practice a center embedded within a business organization where executives could develop and strengthen the mental skills needed to excel under the pressure-filled demands the business world brings. Here, for instance, are five situations you will likely recognize.

YOU ARE BEING PRESSURED TO DELIVER

To meet shareholder expectations, there is a huge emphasis on cost cutting in today's post-recession world, as well as downsizing and delivering results on a smaller budget. Fewer people must do more and more and more. No matter how hard you try, at some point there just is not enough time in the day or the resources to get it all done. This can lead to work overload and feelings of being overwhelmed.

YOUR SKILL REQUIREMENTS AND JOB ASSIGNMENTS ARE RAPIDLY CHANGING

When companies downsize, the surviving workers are typically asked to engage in some tasks with which they are unfamiliar and for which they have not been trained or prepared. Thrust into such situations, your learning curve is steep and your chance of failure high. This can cause you to lose confidence.

YOU HAVE TO WORK ON A TEAM

Companies have come to widely adopt the use of teams as a means for increasing efficiency and productivity. However, you might be more comfortable and highly productive working on your own and not so when placed on a team. You find yourself uneasy with being accountable and responsible for your teammates, and the stress can be counterproductive.

TECHNOLOGY IS TRANSFORMING YOUR WORK

Technology has transformed the ways in which we live, work, and play. With the good, however, comes the bad and the ugly—the emails, voice mails, smartphones, laptops, texts, and so on. In other words, what was supposed to be anywhere, anytime, has become everywhere, all the time. Given a finite amount of time in the day, you might allow the demands from work to creep into your family time. And if your family life is important to you, you push that demand further into your personal time. Eventually you realize that the time you had for doing the things that make you happy—sports, gardening, exercising, or reading—has all been spent. At best, this can lead to guilt when you do choose family and personal time over work. At worst, you can lose a sense of your own individuality.

YOU ARE DEALING WITH
DISCONTINUOUS CHANGE

Continuous change is a natural part of life, as linear as time and somewhat easy to predict and accommodate by growing and developing. Discontinuous change, on the other hand, is sudden, unexpected, and unanticipated, and it catches us by surprise: the sale of your company to one whose interests might not align with yours, a reorganization and redistribution of responsibilities, a boss resigning, an opportunity for advancement that goes to someone else, getting laid off, all for reasons beyond your control but with personal and professional effects. Discontinuous change can create an extended period of loss of direction and purpose, a blurred vision of tomorrow.

The cumulative effect of all the above is a lot of pressure and stress. To be able to survive under these conditions, you have only three courses of action:

1. You can opt out of the situation by quitting. You may have friends who have done this, and maybe they found relief in a different career track altogether. However, for most of us, given our debts, lifestyles, and family responsibilities, this is not a realistic option.
2. You can attempt to eliminate the causes of the stress, but for the most part these are beyond your control and impossible to avoid.
3. You can improve the way you respond to the stress: physiologically, mentally, and emotionally. These responses will determine your level of performance and, eventually, your success both at and away from work while preparing you to counter any future stresses. This is your best course of action.

You might think the best way to respond is by focusing on day-to-day processes, which is what most of today's business books and business consultants advocate. That could mean focusing on something specific, such as your design process, your marketing tactics, or your accounting system. But ask yourself the following question: How has getting the processes right ever made an impact on your business? Of course, an organization has to have the proper processes in place to function efficiently. But efficiency and effectiveness are different from *performance*. What happens at a critical moment can greatly affect your business, and the reaction to the situation is determined by a human, not by a process.

Let's say that you have to make a key sales presentation to a big client, and you are up against five competitors. If you get that business, your life is going to change. But getting that business entails much more than mastering a few processes, such as getting the presentation assembled, printed, and delivered. It means understanding your client's needs. Knowing exactly what you want out of the meeting. Seeing what could go wrong. Having faith in your presentation. And maintaining your cool when your product or ideas are questioned.

All this is easier said than done, so how do you do all these things? It takes a deliberate and systematic approach, which is exactly how I've laid out this book. First, you will learn how recent findings in brain science have unveiled a wealth of information about how the brain works and how we can use that information to succeed. Second, I detail the Five-Point Plan. You will learn in-depth about my performance plan and the five areas you need to work on to grow your mental strength. Finally, I apply the Five-Point Plan to extraordinary performance situations to demonstrate its real-world applications. In the end, this book will help you with the following:

- Gain confidence and self-assuredness that stems from a positive, deliberate, and adaptive thought process.
- Gain greater control and self-regulation when under extreme conditions.
- Develop a razor-sharp focus and concentration amid distractions.
- Realize how you can envision success and then make it happen.
- Understand how to lay out a clear purpose and goals, and set attainable benchmarks for getting there.
- Build an increased capacity for situational awareness, mental agility, learned instinct, and commander's calm.

Throughout the book, you will find stories about people who have used this plan and how it has changed their lives for the better. These stories serve to illustrate how the performance plan works, and they also give you something to strive for in your own practice. Most important, what you learn in this book helps you be more successful in not only your career but the rest of your life as well. You will be mentally healthier, stronger, and able to deal with the ups and downs of life.

1

THE UNTAPPED POWER OF MENTAL STRENGTH

WHAT DOES IT TAKE to be *extraordinary?*
Extraordinary people possess a state of mind and emotional calm that transcend the pressures and challenges of life. They understand the mind–body connection and have trained themselves to possess the mental skills that make it possible to go from good to great. They focus on performance. To attain all this, you must first develop a growth mindset.

As we grow up, we adopt one of two mindsets. Stanford psychologist Carol Dweck describes these mindsets as either fixed or growth-oriented. In a fixed mindset, whatever skills, intelligence, or personality traits we happen to have are believed to be concrete and are not under our control. If you're not inherently smart, tough luck! We are either good at something or not. Interestingly, it is with the best of intentions that a fixed mindset is reinforced; when children are told how smart they are after completing a math problem, they become much more likely to give up when given an unsolvable math problem. It seems that an association between intelligence and outcome is developed (i.e., solving the math problem), instead of the hard work involved in completing the task. This is where the growth mindset is built. In Dweck's research, when she highlighted how hard the children must have worked to solve a problem, they stayed with the task much longer than the "smart" group. You might be wondering how this could be. Well, with a growth mindset, abilities and traits are fluid, and they change based on our efforts. As we develop a growth mindset, we feel more in control of our own destiny and are willing to work hard to try to make success occur. Interestingly, no one is born with a fixed mindset; it is our environments and thoughts that shape our outlooks.

In a classic experiment, Dweck and her colleagues asked young children to complete a set of math problems. After the children finished a preliminary test, the researchers told one group that they must be extremely smart, whereas they told the other group that they must have worked really hard. The results on subsequent (and purposefully unsolvable) tests were remarkable. Children who were told how smart they were gave up almost immediately on the unsolvable problems, while the "hard work" group kept at it for a significant amount of time. It seems that if you are told that you are naturally smart, you associate intelligence with success. Therefore, when you are not successful, you must lack intelligence. That is a hard pill to swallow for a young child! On the other hand, being told that hard work leads to success helps children (or anyone, as you will learn) persevere in difficult situations since they associate their efforts with a successful outcome. One thought, one belief, can change our entire outlook.

What we do in our lives is determined by what we think and how we think. For instance, scientists, researchers, and doctors all used to agree that it was physiologically impossible for humans to break the four-minute-mile record. But once Roger Bannister did it in 1954, twenty-four others broke the four-minute-mile record in the following eight months. Once the possibility was open, those who were capable suddenly could achieve what had always seemed impossible.

One small moment, event, or action can be the tipping point for making the biggest changes. I like to call it going the extra degree. Middle school students learn that at 211 degrees, water is hot, but at 212 degrees, water boils and turns to steam. All it takes to go from water to power is one degree. The same is true for you. What are you capable of? What is the one degree that will take you to another level to make extraordinary things happen?

BE, KNOW, DO

The motto "Be, Know, Do" is a simple yet elegant framework that was developed at West Point and used by the U.S. Army. Traditional corporate learning models have focused primarily on "Know" and "Do." For example, education programs are designed to increase knowledge, and training programs aim to change behavior.

The "Be, Know, Do" framework is different because of that third component: Be. I have found in many organizations a reluctance to even address this element of leadership. Yet peak performance is all about the Be. You must develop yourself as an individual. You must invest in your thoughts to achieve the greatest effect.

Real motivation for success is internal, and it is something you must develop for yourself. You have two choices: Do more of the same things others are doing and do them better, *or* do something new and different. To change, you have to get out of your comfort zone. No new results come from old practices!

This is why self-awareness, self-control, and self-management are essential for achieving exceptional performance. The competencies in my Peak Performance Model are at the heart of self-awareness, self-control, and self-mastery. Gaining a competitive edge is really in your hands.

You can train somebody all day long how to do things the best way, but she has to reach that extra degree on her own: she needs to be aware of what she is thinking and regulate how she is reacting. Some naysayers say a glass-half-full mentality is worthless in the real world. But they do not know the science behind the methodology. When you receive a more in-depth education of how positive thinking affects you physiologically and neurologically, and how negative thinking triggers heightened arousal and the stress response, you begin to believe.

The brain is a powerful organ, and you can let it control you, or you can control it. If you have not learned how to control your mindset, you leave yourself open to distraction by any number of stressors. Once a situation is perceived as a threat, the stress response affects your cognitive function, analytical abilities, and the ability to think clearly and rationally, and your body physically tenses. All negative thinking is detrimental. Our minds and bodies are inherently linked with our behavior, influenced by our expectations. So if your brain anticipates only undesirable outcomes and focuses on what is wrong, then it becomes a self-fulfilling prophecy, and it will direct your body into more danger or activities that reinforce the false perception. On the other hand, if we remain calm and positive, our brains will be able to stay clear, and quick thinking will allow us to respond and perform effectively.

Stress compromises your ability to achieve in any given situation. Knowing how to control that stress and instead focus on the goal is key to becoming a peak performer.

Physically when we experience stress, we feel anxious and breathless. If it really makes your anxiety go through the roof, stress can set off a panic attack. When you have gone through extensive physical training, as many athletes do, you can often fall back on your physical prowess during times of stress and distraction. This will be able to get you through those moments, but only to a certain extent. At some point in our lives, all of us face times when even physical preparedness is not enough to get us over the stress. In these instances, it is our winning mindset—that is, our determination, focus, and perseverance—that helps us succeed.

When you learn how to control your thinking, you can achieve extraordinary results. And I am not talking about the ability to multitask. Inversely, it turns out your achievements are directly determined by how *targeted* you can make your focus, not how many things you can focus on at once (see Chapter 7).

While you can teach people what they need to know to do well in their careers or sports, and you can train them to do things in a certain way, to be truly successful they must explore themselves and understand how they can develop their abilities to be successful. It takes all three components, Be, Know, and Do, and the first is crucial to success.

If you cannot find the positive in a situation, it is time to look at it from a different perspective. Put yourself in a position to gain success. If you let yourself succumb to fear and worry, it undermines motivation.

For example, say a college student has to take a math class, but he feels as if he is bad at math and is afraid he will fail the class. How does such a simple thing as thinking a few negative thoughts manifest itself in real life? This person will go to the class and sit in the back because he is not confident in his abilities and does not want to be called on. He will not listen to the lecture, because what's the point? He is not going to "get it" anyway. He will not ask questions for fear of being ridiculed. All of these actions, or inactions, set him up for what he is the most fearful of: failing. How you *feel* about a situation highly influences how you will *achieve* in that situation.

So how do you change your mindset, and allow the Be to take over? How can you react in a situation where you historically have felt nervous and hesitant and stressed, and achieve great things?

We start by turning around a situation that you are looking to change. Ask yourself the following question: If a close friend or family member was facing a similar challenge or situation, how would you advise her or him to solve it? You would be surprised at how the ideas start to flow.

Then ask yourself: Now why can't I use those ideas for me?

What has your thinking gotten you up to this point? Failure? A glass-half-empty mindset? Open yourself up to the possibility that you are not doing all you can to achieve your goals.

PERFORMANCE TRANSFORMATIONS

I have seen some big successes from our company's work with veterans. As a retired U.S. Army colonel and Vietnam veteran, it is very important to me that we help our servicemen and servicewomen as much as we can.

At Apex Performance, our programs with veterans help soldiers transition from the military to civilian careers. Many of them worry they will not know how to do a job well, or that they do not have the right background or training for the job. All of this creates stress. When they were in the military, they did not have to worry about knowing how to do a job because they were provided training. Many of them thought they would be in the military forever until an injury meant they could no longer serve.

The trainers at Apex are able to give the veterans a

different kind of message than what has been stopping them from moving on. They convey to them that, as former soldiers, they are coming in with a lot of strengths. We tell them, "You have the advantage. You understand leadership from a whole different perspective. You have skills you can't learn in a book, and you've got experience other people don't have." After learning how to manage their thoughts, the way they look at a situation, their emotions, and their stressors, they improve their performance.

For some, transitioning to the civilian world also means dealing with the effects of a traumatic brain injury (TBI) or post-traumatic stress disorder (PTSD). Many come in discouraged by the effects of these conditions, but we tell them how powerful the brain is. Just because you have TBI or PTSD does not mean you cannot ace the test or find a way to succeed. You can retrain the brain to make up for what was lost.

The power of the human brain goes far beyond positive thinking. We show the inspiring story of Jody Miller to veterans, people with TBI, or warriors and athletes who have not been diagnosed with brain injuries but show symptoms.

Jody Miller was a typical, healthy, active toddler. Then, shortly after her third birthday, she began having debilitating seizures. Diagnosed with Rasmussen's syndrome, she eventually lost control of her left side and was having seizures so often she could not function normally. Her pediatric neurologist determined the best treatment was to surgically remove the entire right half of Jody's brain. This sounded like a drastic measure, but if it would help Jody, her parents were willing to give their permission for the surgery.

Within days of the surgery, Jody was walking and talking. By using exercises to train the left part of her brain to control the left side of her body, Jody now runs, plays, and dances just like the other children at her school. There is minimal evidence of her previous paralysis.

Jody is a living example of the brain's ability to compensate, to make new connections, and to adapt after trauma. After a brain injury, you are still able to do what you have always done; you might just have to do it differently.

The same ability to compensate is true for amputees. It is important for them to know they can still get from point A to point B rather than giving up. It might take prosthetics or devices and learning how to adapt to a new situation, but our brains give us the ability to adjust and thrive and be successful. The power of the brain to adapt plays a huge part in our ability to overcome what life throws at us. Until you have achieved the highest level of control possible over your thoughts, feelings, and actions, you cannot hope to achieve peak performance levels. One of the key elements of self-mastery is fully recognizing what you can and cannot control. Peak performers put all their energy and effort into what they can control, while letting go of the things they have no control over.

Here is a story I use to demonstrate this theory. One evening, an elderly Cherokee told his grandson about a battle that goes on inside all people. He said, "My son, the battle is between two wolves inside us. One is evil. It is fear, anger, jealousy, regret, greed, self-pity, guilt, resentment, superiority, and ego. It carries anxiety, concern, uncertainty, indecision, and inaction.

"The other wolf is good. It is joy, peace, hope, humility, kindness, benevolence, empathy, truth, compassion, and faith. It brings, calm, conviction, confidence, enthusiasm, and action."

The grandson thought about it for a moment, then meekly asked his grandfather, "Which wolf wins?"

The old Cherokee replied, "The one you feed."

Courage is not the absence of fear—it is the realization that something else is more important. Confidence, positive thinking, and understanding that we have the power inside us to change ourselves and change our outcomes can make a difference in our performance. All that preparation leads you to the point to be ready for the life-changing moment that makes the biggest impact, that one defining moment that takes you to another level.

It does not matter where you are in your life; you can rewire your brain and function in ways you never thought you could. By learning the skills necessary to set goals and focus your attention, you will be able to make good decisions even during stressful times and perform at your best under intense pressure. So let's assess where your mental strengths are. Then I will walk you through the specific steps to improving them that I developed through my own experiences and research.

2

ASSESSING YOUR MENTAL STRENGTHS

THE FRAMEWORK WE USE for teaching and developing peak performance mental skills was derived from an extensive search of the literature on peak performance found in sports and performance psychology journals, by studying exceptional performers in extreme conditions, and through our own experience with the peak performers we have helped develop over the years. This model was derived by investigating not only what peak performers do in extreme conditions but also how they do it from a mental perspective. Our peak performance framework has five parts, which are referred to as core mental skills: goal setting, adaptive thinking, stress and energy management, attention control, and imagery.

Before I discuss each of these skills, what they mean, how they can be developed, and their impact on performance and life in general, I would like you to take an assessment I call a Desired Behaviors Inventory, which will identify what your strengths are and where you could use some work. You may already use imagery or goal setting, or you may find that you have not used these tools as effectively as you could and will be able to pick out the areas that need the most work as you read through this section. As you spend time taking this assessment, focus on both the areas you know you need to work on and skills you already use, so you can continue doing what works. Then, at the end of the book, reflect on what you still need to practice and work on.

PEAK PERFORMANCE SKILLS LEVEL SELF-ASSESSMENT

Assess your level of mastery of the five peak performance skills described below by selecting the response that best describes your current level of proficiency. Rate each item on a scale from 1 to 5.

Never   Sometimes   Always
1   2   3   4   5

GOAL SETTING   SCORE _____

1 2 3 4 5   I have a clear vision and mission.

1 2 3 4 5   I systematically write down my goals and objectives.

1 2 3 4 5   I act on my goals and objectives.

1 2 3 4 5   My goals and objectives are present in my mind.

1 2 3 4 5   I reassess my goals.

ADAPTIVE THINKING   SCORE _____

1 2 3 4 5   I am aware of what I say to myself.

1 2 3 4 5   I can stop negative thoughts on command and replace them with positive thoughts.

1 2 3 4 5   I know what to say to myself to build and maintain confidence.

1 2 3 4 5   I know how I need to think and what to say to myself to influence my performance.

1 2 3 4 5   I use what I think and say to myself to influence my behavior and performance.

STRESS MANAGEMENT   SCORE _____

1 2 3 4 5   I regularly listen to my body to know whether I am too wired or flat.

1 2 3 4 5   I know how to make my mind and body feel to perform optimally.

1 2 3 4 5   I do relaxation exercises that calm me down within seconds.

1 2 3 4 5   I know the key recovery activities that allow me to recover from stressful days.

1 2 3 4 5   I use the key recovery activities that allow me to recover from stressful days.

ATTENTION CONTROL   SCORE _____

1 2 3 4 5   I am able to concentrate on a task for the needed duration.

1 2 3 4 5   If interrupted during a task, I can get myself back on track.

1 2 3 4 5   I know how to pay attention to listen effectively.

1 2 3 4 5   I can shift my attention from the big picture to the details and back or vice versa.

1 2 3 4 5   I know exactly where to pay attention in a given task.

VISUALIZATION AND IMAGERY   SCORE _____

1 2 3 4 5   I can literally see pictures in my mind.

1 2 3 4 5   I can control the images I create in my mind.

1 2 3 4 5   The pictures I create in my mind are clear and vivid.

1 2 3 4 5   I use pictures in my mind to rehearse future
business scenarios.

1 2 3 4 5   I create a clear picture of the desired outcome
so that others can "see" it, too.

OVERALL SCORE _____

When you see the score for each of the different sections, you will be able
to assess which parts of the five-point model you need to work on.

Score 16–25: You are doing a great job maximizing your performance.
Now keep it up. Use these concepts and techniques in all areas of your
life to take yourself to the next level.

Score 10–15: You are headed in the right direction but need to practice these skills on a consistent basis. Just like anything you learn, the
more you practice, the more likely you are to stick to it.

Score 5–9: You are not taking control of your performance, and you
allow the performance situation to control you. It may be OK when
things are going well, but it probably hurts when you need it most.
Work at it and take back control.

3

THE FIVE-POINT PLAN FOR PLAN FOR LEADERSHIP AND PERFORMANCE EXCELLENCE

3

THE FIVE-POINT PLAN FOR LEADERSHIP AND PERFORMANCE EXCELLENCE

THE KEY ASPECT OF superior performance is inner control: control over the mental, emotional, and physiological states that are present in every performance situation. That control is exercised through well-developed peak performance competencies. Without mastery of these, business professionals cannot hope to repeat and sustain exceptional performance under pressure without the inevitable consequences on leadership effectiveness, team and organizational performance, and, ultimately, their own health and welfare.

So what are these critical mental skills that can build and develop the performance capacities essential for extraordinary performance in extreme conditions? What are some of the discoveries from the new science of the brain that affect how we develop these mental skills and how we view the mind in general? Systematic education and training in these skill sets develops the power of purpose, optimism, self-control, self-regulation, focus, and imagination.

This is done by developing the five skills of the Apex Model (figure 3.1)

Figure 3.1 Apex Performance Model.

1. GOAL SETTING

Oliver Wendell Holmes said, "The greatest thing in this world is not so much where we are, but in what direction we are moving." A journey starts with knowing where you want to end up. This is especially true for anyone who wants to begin the journey to becoming a peak performer. Setting goals is relatively easy. Making them happen is not. A key part of any lasting goal-setting process is the idea of a mission. Knowing and living a mission provides the motivation and perseverance to forge ahead when the going gets tough. It is much more than having a goal.

A great deal has been written about goal setting and goal-setting techniques. Our approach to setting the target is not so much about a technique as it is a process for identifying what you really want to accomplish, the inclusive smaller steps needed to get there, and the positive mindset necessary for ensuring enduring determination. This last part is critical. Stopping with a list of goals and objectives is just not enough. It does not activate the energy needed to see them through to completion. They must be deliberately connected to our daily thoughts and self-talk. It takes transforming objectives, which in their simplest forms are actions, into affirmations that connect what we are doing with what we are thinking. By recording these affirmations and having people listen to them regularly, we mimic the way young children learn language at home—hearing it repeatedly, creating new neural pathways.

After completing our goal-setting process, a CEO of a $3 billion healthcare company said, "I have done goal-setting exercises before. We in business do this all the time. But taking it to the next level is something I had not done before. The power of this process is truly remarkable."

2. ADAPTIVE THINKING

Confidence is the ultimate determinant of success. It comes from within. No one can give it to you. It reflects how we view ourselves and how prepared we see ourselves for oncoming challenges. We see and hear this all the time in sports, but we do not hear it as much in the business world. Yet our experience in working with business leaders has shown us that confidence can be a crucial issue.

We become what we think about most. People carry around images of themselves—of who they are and how they perform. These "pictures" begin at birth and continue throughout life, capturing all of our experiences. These experiences reflect both our successes and failures, as well as the manner in which they are interpreted and stored. Much of this self-image is driven by our thoughts (positive and negative) and maintained and reinforced by our self-talk. Given the basic negativism surrounding our lives, being positive and having trust and confidence in our abilities is really hard work.

Our brains do not help here, either. There are areas in the old brain stem (primitive brain) whose sole function is to magnify negative incoming messages and minimize positive ones. To make matters worse, the limbic system, which is the seat of emotions, floods us with negative emotions and perceptions with the primary task of predicting the worst. These brain functions are a carryover from our prehistoric days in the African savanna and function as if we were still there. From the moment of birth, the deck is somewhat stacked against us. Fighting these built-in mechanisms with our logical, thinking brains is an ongoing struggle. We can learn to shift from negative to positive patterns of thinking and to control that chatter inside our heads. People need to take responsibility for their thoughts, and deliberate and systematic training can help them achieve that control.

We train people to shift from negative to positive patterns of thinking and to control self-talk. Based on Martin Seligman's work and other recent scientific evidence based on how children learn language at home, positive-effective thinking can be systematically developed. We help the individual come up with affirmations and then record them to listen to repeatedly. This methodology is derived from research, and it is an effective tool for transforming negative thoughts to positive ones and moving from a pessimistic to an optimistic mindset. Mastery of this competence can transform a person into an exceptional thinker.

3. STRESS AND ENERGY MANAGEMENT

Stress and energy go together. Anyone can perform well when everything is going just right. But what about when conditions are unfavorable, when things are going against you, when the pressure is on, when things are not going according to plan? Who really delivers then? There are performers who actually thrive under these conditions. They welcome the pressure. It drives them and gives them energy and desire, coupled with the ultimate satisfaction of having overcome all odds while doing something exceptional. These are your peak performers. The debilitating effects of stress on the individual and the organization have been well documented in recent years. There is little debate, for example, that for business organizations, stress is a major factor that reveals itself as diminished performance and increased healthcare costs. As another example, in the war on terror, stress manifests itself especially in the form of increased rates of PTSD and related psychological disorders.

One of the major stressors in business is the relentless pressure to deliver results through higher and higher levels of performance and ever-increasing productivity. Many companies offer stress management seminars in hopes of raising awareness about the effects of stress and providing simple coping mechanisms. However, research on high performers in both sports and the military has shown that the ability to handle oneself in high-pressure situations is less about the stressors and more about the individual's response to them. The U.S. Army recognizes that the challenges of combat can inevitably produce stress in a soldier. Emerging understanding of the physical and mental reactions of humans to stress suggest that while stress is a natural and inevitable reaction to extreme environments and events, it need not be debilitating to the individual or the unit.[1] The solution lies in a more systematic and integrated approach to providing the necessary tools for actually thriving under pressure, not just surviving.

We couple traditional stress management techniques with innovative uses of the most recent sensory feedback technologies to develop the ability to manage stress and energy levels. We agree with John Eliot. He points out in his book, *Overachievement*, that exceptional performances are not about being relaxed. They are about being energized and excited and impassioned and always very much in control. Understanding how stress works from a neurophysiological perspective, having means at your disposal for altering its effects, and receiving quality high-tech feedback on how you are doing are powerful tools for learning how to thrive in pressure situations and for living your life.

4. ATTENTION CONTROL

In their insightful book *The Attention Economy*, Thomas Davenport and John Beck discuss how in today's society "the new scarcest resource isn't ideas or talent, but attention itself."[2] The demand for our attention in modern society is unparalleled in both scope and intensity. Yet the way in which we attend has not significantly changed over time.

We still primarily learn to attend to the right things at the right time through trial and error and, if fortunate, through good coaching by parents, teachers, coaches, and so forth. Through this method, we learn what is useful for our attention and what is not as we encounter new situations. However, today's stimulus-rich environment, with so many different things competing for our attention, does not provide the most efficient and effective atmosphere in which to learn to attend. The resultant attention deficit threatens to seriously cripple the workplace. In fact, a new term has been coined by Davenport and Beck—*Organizational ADD*, a condition wherein there is "an increased likelihood for missing key information when making decisions, diminished time for reflection . . . difficulty holding others' attention . . . and decreased ability to focus when necessary."[3]

If you think about it, today's business world seems to call for the type of attention required on a battlefield, and in a battlefield environment, we must change the way we develop the ability to focus and concentrate. We need to place less emphasis on *what* to pay attention to and more on teaching *how* to pay attention. A more scientific approach to addressing attention is to recognize that it is the result of a number of different brain areas at work, and we must train these areas to search for and integrate new information with the old. The complexity of these crossover signals provides some insight on how the brain filters incoming information. Without this filtering process, we would be overwhelmed and unable to survive.

Our brains are wired to attend to one thing in one sensory mode at any one moment. This explains a little known and rarely accepted fact: There is no multitasking! By *multitasking*, I mean simultaneous execution of at least two or more tasks. Actually, this should read, "There is no multiattending!" Our brains simply are not set up to do that. Habitual multitasking may even result in a situation where you cannot focus even if you want to. Even though multitasking is a myth, in a survey conducted by Apex Performance, 67 percent of the responders considered themselves good at it. What you can do is learn to shift your focus and concentration in a way that improves your ability to attend to what matters most. What people perceive as multitasking is actually an efficient shifting of attention between senses and targets.

Highly effective attention requires complete immersion with a singular focus and sustained intensity. Yes, we can physically execute a number of different tasks simultaneously, but the quality of each will be severely diminished. You can easily observe this for yourself when driving and texting or even talking on a cell phone, when answering emails while engaged in a telephone conversation and typing a memo, and so on. The list is endless.

We provide business leaders and others an innovative and scientific approach to addressing this attention challenge. Our attention control training combines a simple but robust framework for understanding how attention works, a means for navigating that framework, and new brain wave (EEG) technology that provides accurate feedback about how one is paying attention—the key to improving focus and concentration directly.

5. IMAGERY

In its simplest form, imagery is about doing a mental recon and rehearsal in a very specific way. To achieve a challenging goal, you must see it already accomplished. Imagery, commonly referred to as *visualization,* is a powerful tool for doing exactly that. It involves using all the senses to create or re-create an experience in the mind. Everyone has this inherent capability; how well it is developed is a function of your developmental experiences. We all use imagery in one form or another all the time. We differ in its sophistication and effectiveness. Some visualize effectively with no formal training, while most do so only after systematic training and practice. The neurological wiring, however, is in everyone. The early and consistent use of imagination in play and work helps build the brain "muscles" for visualizing. Imagery maximizes potential for performance by helping develop greater confidence, energy, concentration, and feelings of success.

In our Five-Point Peak Performance Model, visualization and imagery are developed as a specific peak performance competency as well as an integrating mechanism. Imagery can be developed as a powerful mental talent that can be used to enhance performance, improve a specific skill, accelerate healing and recovery from injury, generate breakthrough ideas, and create a vision. The first step is assessing how well an individual's visualization skill has developed. We have discovered through biofeedback and neurofeedback instrumentation that high-quality visualization is characterized by a deep physiological and mental coherence coupled with an optimal level of alertness and concentration. The power of imagery comes from the confidence gained by seeing and feeling successful performance in the mind before it actually happens. The common description of seeing success in your mind beforehand is the thought "I have been here before."

IN-DEPTH LOOK AT TRAINING

An in-depth look at the science behind the development and application of our five-point model will show how these processes work in all facets of life.

My initial theory was that a multifaceted training

regimen would enhance resilience, self-confidence, adaptability, and mental agility. The key element was the integrated use of the latest biofeedback and neuroscience technologies for accelerating the acquisition and application of training. Technology brings to life all performance theories and translates progress into real-time statistics.

Today I use this same biofeedback at Apex. Professionals can record vital data in real experience conditions and review them afterward with their clients. Each person who comes to our offices takes a baseline assessment at the beginning of the program and then completes one-on-one sessions with our Peak Performance Training professional. Our goal is to create a person who is well equipped with a variety of strategies that will enable him to thrive within the constant pressures of his world. In order to accomplish this, a holistic and systematic approach regarding breathing, heart rate, blood flow, muscle tension, activation levels, and brain wave activity needs to occur. A person starts with gaining self-awareness for each modality required in an ideal performance state. Next, she learns specific strategies for how to be in command of her brain and body, and how to rewire her system for managing high-pressure maneuvers. Finally, a person's newly acquired and enhanced performance state is tested in a variety of situations until he can demonstrate mastery, trusting his body will appropriately and consistently respond in the most effective manner.

When embedded in an organization, we install a brain-training program we call a "Mindroom." In addition to one-on-one training, those in this program are responsible for daily brain-training exercises proven to advance performance. The Mindroom is uniquely designed to offer self-driven, controlled, repetitive practice that acts as reinforcement for what clients learn in their individual sessions. Mental skills that can be gained include rapid, efficient scanning of important/relevant information, short-term memory recall, and quick comparison and processing of visual information. Particular programs target speed and accuracy in handling information to develop greater mental clarity, quickness, and focus. The purpose is to react as quickly as possible while still achieving high levels of precision. Overall brain function related to flexibility and problem solving also greatly improves.

Progress is tracked and measured throughout the year, detailing where each participant is in regard to achieving optimal levels. This tangible, data-driven training allows the client to know exactly where her current level of functioning is and to be able to set goals for each physiological and mental peak performance domain.

NEURO TRAINING

One of the unique aspects of Apex training is that, through EEGs, we are able to analyze brain wave activity and report significant changes in attention levels and focused state. Seeing in more detail exactly how the brain functions in performance situations, we can then create more of the positive brain waves we want and diminish the brain waves we do not desire.

This type of brain training has the potential to improve performance, learning ability, and confidence by affecting arousal, attentional processes, and self-regulation. Brain wave frequencies are associated with different mental states. Through neurofeedback, we are able to discern the client's level of focus and executive function. In addition, we can teach the brain to increase its production of situationally beneficial brain waves or decrease the production of detrimental wave states so participants can exercise greater control.

ACCOUNTABILITY

Committing time and effort to learning how the mind influences performance and making important connections between mind and body will enable Special Operations warriors, athletes, and business leaders to achieve their best when it matters most. But how do you know if it is really effective?

As in any training and development process, quality and accurate feedback are essential for learning. Since peak performance competencies are internal, learning to master them is best achieved with advanced biofeedback and neurofeedback technologies that measure covert activities like heart rate variability, respiration, blood pressure, brain activity, and so on. These technologies were once the domain of clinicians and biofeedback therapists, but we now use them to provide accurate and measurable feedback as the individual learns to master control over mental, physiological, and emotional responses to demanding and challenging events. Research in performance psychology continues to validate the importance and effectiveness of the competencies depicted in our five-point model.

TRAIN YOUR BRAIN

Recent discoveries provide amazing insights into how the brain works and its direct influence on performance. These discoveries alter the way we view learning. Two findings that will surely change what and the way we teach and train are neurogenesis and neuroplasticity. *Neurogenesis* is the process whereby neurons divide and propagate, just like cells in the rest of the body. New discoveries about the brain's ability to generate and regenerate neural connections demolish the long-standing "science" that the brain cells with which we are born are all that we get and no new cells are grown. *Neuroplasticity* is the brain's ability to change its structure through experience. It is not a fixed entity. Environmental factors do not just influence the brain; they actually alter its structure and thus change it permanently. The implications of this discovery for educating and training are profound. Neuroplasticity plays a vital role in learning. Lifelong learning is now a reality, right to the very end. This new science tells us that the brain is not static but a living, evolving, constantly changing organ.

By literally training the brain, we can significantly develop the mental skills needed to create the leader capacities essential for success in the *new world*. Computerized "brain games" provide sophisticated exercises designed to directly affect certain brain functions and the mental processes associated with them. These complex mental processes influence and drive everything we do. Caution must be exercised when deciding to use any of the readily available brain games. Many of the games and the sites that sell them are gimmicky and do not work. Legitimate brain exercises must come from well-researched software and hardware that are properly developed by cognitive psychologists and neuroscientists.

For the brain to be stimulated and grow from these new and challenging exercises, it needs a specific pathway to follow. Chapter 4 walks you through how to develop an action plan that will break down what you need to accomplish, by the daily behaviors you will employ, to reach that higher level of performance. This timeline will keep you accountable and direct your progress toward all that you want to achieve.

4

GOAL SETTING

T IS EASY TO keep wandering down different paths when you are looking to improve your performance. Often we try many different things, questioning if the path we are on is the right one, and our doubt and uncertainty make us take a wrong turn. That is why setting goals is important to success, and it is the first component of our performance model.

You might think setting goals is easy. We all have things in life we want, whether it is getting that big promotion, owning our own homes, or running a 5K. Actually reaching those goals is much more difficult. Having a systematic goal-setting process and plan encourages people to keep their eyes on the prize. Striving to get to that end goal should be viewed as an ongoing process of continuous change and adaptation.

Think of setting and achieving goals as more of a GPS system than a roadmap for your life. A roadmap is a static object, but a GPS system constantly adapts. It alerts when you might encounter traffic, road construction, or other hazards and delays, and it will reset your path for you. The same is true for performance at work, at home, or in sports. Your boss may change, the corporation may be restructured, you might get assigned to a new team, or you might have an injury that upsets your ability to practice. Understanding and living day-to-day with clear goals provides the passion and motivation to persevere, even when obstacles get in the way. A journey starts with knowing where you want to end up. An integral part of any lasting goal-setting process is the idea of a mission. Having a mission is much more than just setting a goal. It is deciding what you want out of your life. The approach to setting your target outcome identifies what you really want to accomplish and helps you figure out the inclusive smaller steps needed to get there while maintaining the positive mindset necessary for ensuring enduring determination.

Goal setting has been a part of my personal strategy for success for a long time. I realized at a young age that having something to work toward helped keep my mind on the task at hand and get to the end result faster than I probably would without a clear goal.

When I was a boy in Hungary after World War II, part of my father's job was driving American soldiers around. While he was focused on earning the money that would let us emigrate to America, I was inspired by the soldiers' bravery and camaraderie and became focused on one day attending West Point. After we moved to Pennsylvania, I told my high school guidance counselor about this dream. He dismissed it, saying I would never achieve it. I nevertheless applied my senior year—and I was rejected. I did not have the necessary nomination. But I did not give up. After two years at Valley Forge Military Academy & College, I applied again, now knowing what was necessary for the application process. I was accepted. It was one of the defining moments of my life.

Later, following my tour of duty in Vietnam, I was assigned to attend graduate school for two years to earn my master's degree in preparation for my role on the faculty at West Point. While there, my faculty adviser offered me the opportunity to earn a doctorate in psychology and leadership in the time the army had allotted for me to do my graduate work. It meant a much heavier workload than the other graduate students had, including advanced research and data collection. I knew this was an opportunity I could not pass up, so I seized the moment. I set my goal, worked hard, and returned to West Point with a Ph.D. in just two and a half years.

Setting goals is the first step in achieving success, and sometimes the goals you set can end up being a turning point in your life or career. You may have heard of Lou Holtz, one of the winningest football coaches in American college history. He had a great career, but he started out young and inexperienced just like the rest of us. Part of what made Lou Holtz so successful was that he learned early on in his career the importance of setting goals.

In 1966, Lou Holtz served as an assistant coach at the University of South Carolina.[1] He was there for one year when the head coach left for another position, and Holtz found himself without a job. His wife was pregnant with their third child. Instead of complaining about their dire situation, his wife gave him a book, *The Magic of Thinking Big*, by David Schwartz. The book said if you are bored in life, if you do not wake up with a burning desire to get up and do something in the morning, the main problem is you do not have any goals. To be really accurate at goal setting, you need to take a piece of paper and pencil and write down all the things you wish to do. So Lou started a list, which included the following:

- Go to the White House for dinner.
- Go on *The Tonight Show*.
- Meet the Pope.
- Go to football conferences and win championships.
- Shoot a hole in one.
- Coach Notre Dame.

There were 101 other items on Holtz's list. Full of excitement, Holtz showed them to his wife, telling her, "We're going to do every one of them." She said, "You need another one: 108—get a job."

Holtz achieved at least some of his goals. Since making that list in 1966, he has taken over five college coaching situations. He never inherited a winning football team, yet by his second year of coaching, each of his teams went to a bowl game. He coached Notre Dame, and he even made it on *The Tonight Show*.

This man's story is incredibly inspiring, and it captures the magic of having goals. They not only give us something to work toward but can provide us with the motivation and energy to keep going, even when times are tough.

OUTCOME GOALS

The first step in goal setting is to define your outcome goals. These are the big things you want to strive for in life, such as success in your career, running a marathon, writing a book, or traveling on all seven continents. These are goals that take time to be accomplished and cannot be rushed.

When setting your outcome goals, remember the acronym SMART: Specific, Measurable, Achievable, Realistic, and Timely.

SPECIFIC

A specific goal has a much greater chance of being accomplished than a general goal does. Answer the six "W" questions to make sure your goal is specific. Who: Determine who is involved. What: Define what you want to accomplish. Where: Identify a location. When: Establish a time frame. Which: Identify requirements and constraints. Why: Specify the reasons, purpose, or benefits of accomplishing the goal.

MEASURABLE

Establish concrete criteria for measuring progress toward attaining your goal. Measuring your progress helps you stay on track, reach target dates, and experience achievement.

ACHIEVABLE

You can attain almost any goal you set when you plan your steps wisely and establish a time frame that allows you to carry out those steps. You develop the attitude, skills, and financial capacity to reach them. When you write your goals down, you build your self-image, seeing yourself as worthy of these goals, and you develop the traits and personality that allow you to possess them.

REALISTIC

A goal must represent an objective toward which you are willing and able to work. A goal can be both high and realistic; you are the only one who can decide just how high your goal should be. Some of the hardest jobs you ever accomplished actually might have seemed easy at the time, simply because they were a labor of love. Your goal is probably realistic if you truly believe it can be accomplished.

TIMELY

A goal should be grounded within a certain time frame. If you want to lose ten pounds, when do you want to lose it by? "Someday" will not work. If you anchor it within a specific time frame, say, by May 1, you have set your unconscious mind into motion to begin working on the goal.

SPECIFIC GOALS

There are seven simple steps to effectively set specific goals.

1. DEFINE YOUR DREAM

Take a moment and ask yourself the following questions:

- What accomplishments, achievements, or experiences would be worth your best effort?
- What would you attempt if you knew it was impossible to fail?
- What would you go for if you could put your heart and soul into just one thing?

2. KNOW WHERE YOU ARE RIGHT NOW

Evaluate your current situation. What do you like about it? What would you change?

3. DECIDE WHAT YOU NEED TO DEVELOP

Remember that you do not have to change everything all at once. That can be overwhelming. Look over your list of possibilities and pick one that you feel most excited about. Start there and save the list for the second round, after you achieve the first item.

4. PLAN FOR STEADY IMPROVEMENT

You need to grow and develop your goal behaviors. Keep raising the bar with the progress you make and pushing yourself to the next level as you step closer to your final goal.

5. SET AND PURSUE SHORT-TERM GOALS

Breaking your overall goal into smaller chunks makes it seem more doable and keeps your motivation high as you reach these mini-goals along the way.

6. COMMIT YOURSELF COMPLETELY

Make sure the goal you are working on is something you really want, not just something that sounds good. Then find creative ways to stumble across that goal on a daily basis.

7. CONTINUALLY MONITOR YOUR PROGRESS

Review, evaluate, adjust, and amend your action plan on a regular basis so you can keep moving in a positive direction. If it is too easy, challenge yourself by increasing the workload or difficulty. If you are struggling, identify the obstacles getting in your way and revise your approach and what it is going to take to get you there.

THE APEX APPROACH

The Apex goal-setting process is a tool for identifying what you want to accomplish. It gives you the critical steps needed to get there while maintaining the positive mindset essential for enduring determination. Possessing a list of goals and objectives is not enough. It does not activate the energy needed to see them through to completion. They must be deliberately connected to our daily thoughts and self-talk, which is why we incorporate positive affirmations such as "I am an effective leader" or "I deserve to be happy." For example, if you want to work out in the mornings more often, you could put a Post-it note on your alarm clock/phone every night that says something like "You got this!" or "You are healthy and fit!" If you want a promotion, you could make sure to have a reminder to talk to someone outside your department at work every day to gain exposure and network. When we see our goals and hear our goals, we are reminded to actually do something to move toward them *right now.*

Goals give individuals control in situations where they have little. For instance, a low-level employee cannot change the large company where he is not enjoying working simply through his actions. But he can change himself. He can make himself more marketable, more appealing; he can achieve sales goals and get good performance reviews. He can become a better public speaker, learn new computer skills, network with other workers inside and outside the company. Having an identified objective—for example, to get a new job—can help by directing our attention to a specific task, mobilizing and prolonging our effort and intensity, encouraging resilience and perseverance in the face of adversity, and facilitating the development of new problem-solving strategies.

Two important steps in setting outcome goals are the following:

1. Have a clear vision and mission, and be able to articulate both.
2. Be able to translate that mission into outcome, performance, and process goals.

The process takes you from your "dream" to clear actions that have to be taken to reach your goals. It involves developing the necessary commitment, evaluating potential barriers to goal attainment and working through them, constructing action plans that take you step-by-step toward your goal, obtaining objective feedback, evaluating progress, and reinforcing achievement through positive affirmation aids, such as "I am in control of what I think, say, and do," and "Each day I get stronger."

PERFORMANCE GOALS

These are the things you need to do to help you reach your outcome goal. These are specific areas where you need to focus that will help you get where you want to be.

PROCESS GOALS

Once you have set your performance goals, it is time to think of the process that you have to go through to meet them. What skills, abilities, and knowledge do you need? These are things you do on a daily or weekly basis to achieve performance goals.

When setting goals, remember the following:

- Small goals are more important than big goals.
- All goals are *real* goals, and they must be written down.
- A goal should be written as an end state and as positive end statements (statements representing what or how you will be when you complete or achieve that goal, i.e., *My outcome goal is completing a marathon in under three hours*).

PUTTING IT ALL TOGETHER

Let's take a look at Dave's goals as an example. Dave's outcome goal is to get a promotion to regional sales manager. His performance goals are what he needs to do to get the promotion. Dave decides to refine his presentation skills, reach a set sales goal, and achieve high customer service ratings.

Process goals are the steps Dave takes in order to make his performance goals. He takes a class at his local library on PowerPoint to learn new tricks to making a great presentation. He practices sample dialogues with his other team members to make more sales. They meet weekly, over lunch, and role-play. Finally, he spends hours learning the product line and delivery system accurately to improve his customer service skills.

All of this works together to help Dave reach one outcome goal: a promotion.

Here are two other examples of processes and performance goals that lead to accomplishing an outcome goal.

OUTCOME GOAL: HAVE A SECURE AND HAPPY FAMILY
▶ First Performance Goal: Generate a Positive Environment for My Children

Process goals:
- I spend time individually with each child.
- I manage my stress levels daily.
- I accept my children as they are daily.
- I smile as much as possible around my children.
- I review positive things every week with my children.

▶ Second Performance Goal: Strengthen My Marriage

Process goals:
- I control my body language daily.
- I schedule a date night once a week.
- I communicate effectively.
- I show compassion.

By setting goals and being mindful of his actions, this husband and father was able to reach his outcome of having a secure and happy family.

Here is another example of setting goals in practice and how you would go about setting up your performance and process goals.

OUTCOME GOAL: GET A 4.0 GPA IN THE NEXT SEMESTER

Note: if you are starting with a C average and want to move straight into an A average, this might be a little unrealistic and too fast a turnaround time. The goal must be attainable. So your first outcome goal would be to get a B average if you are starting with a C.

Performance goals:
- I manage my time and get organized (time management).
- I am prepared and present for every class (class participation).
- I turn in my assignments on time (effective learning and study skills).

Process goals:
- Write a daily checklist—look at very specific action-oriented behaviors, and dial in on what it is going to take each and every day to get to the performance goal and finally to achieve your outcome goal. Lay the groundwork specifically.

- I keep a calendar for when assignments are due.
- I raise my hand to participate in class every session.
- I assign myself times to study and read what I need to.

Look through those checklists and assess yourself honestly. Say you were late turning in assignments twice because you stayed up with your friends and pushed the snooze button one too many times. If that is the case, you might resolve not to go out on school nights. You might not have allocated enough time for studying, and gotten a C when you were striving for a B. If so, make notes to study longer in preparation for the next test. The process is all about constantly evaluating yourself and doing what you need to do to get back on track.

PERSONAL AFFIRMATIONS FOR POSITIVE EFFECTIVE THINKING

Your list of goals and objectives must be deliberately connected to your ongoing thoughts and become a part of the daily "chatter" in your head. There is a systematic method for doing exactly that. Transforming performance objectives, which in their simplest form are actions, into daily thoughts connects what we are thinking with what we are doing. It is the way the mind–body connection operates best.

Transforming goals into affirmations, which is something positive that you tell yourself, helps connect what we are *doing* with what we are *thinking*. For instance, Dave would not want to be practicing his sales presentations and doing his other process goals, all the while thinking, "I'm going to be stuck in this job forever." He needs to have positive affirmations to bolster all his hard work. You can help create a positive mindset by recording affirmations onto a CD or on your phone and listening to them regularly. This practice mimics the way young children learn language at home—hearing it repeatedly creates new neural pathways in the brain for success.

If the key to achieving goals is getting into the right mindset, how do you write effective affirmations to get you there? An affirmation should always be about what you want as opposed to what you do not want. It should feature the following elements:

- Personal inclusion: You should be an integral part of the affirmative reminder.
- Present tense: State the behavior as if you were already doing it or it has been achieved.
- Use "feeling" words: Certain words evoke your emotions more than others.
- Practicality: Use realistic standards like "consistently, "regularly," and so on, and do not use inflexible ones that speak of perfection, such as "always," "every time," and so on.

- Do not compare yourself with others: Do not say, "I'm going to beat Trish to the top." Instead, use a standard for comparison, not the behavior or achievement of others.
- Sustainable action: It requires continuity and a period of time to do it, not a one-off action.

Here are some examples of positive affirmations:

- I am in control of what I think, say, and do.
- My thoughts stay in the moment.
- My breathing is deep and relaxed.
- I allow myself time to grow into the role.
- I create an organized workday.
- I eat healthy meals.
- I am interested in what others have to say.
- I am an effective leader.
- I persevere.
- I advocate for myself, what I want, and what I need.
- I am successful in life and work.
- I am positive.
- I am confident.

Can the power of positive thinking really get us through, even when our physical strength is compromised? The answer is yes. One of the most amazing hiking stories of all time is proof of just how powerful the brain can be. Climbers Joe Simpson and Simon Yates were attempting to climb the Siula Grande in the Peruvian Andes when Simpson slid on a glacier and crushed his tibia. Yates could have left him there to die, but instead he chose to try to take him with him, and that choice led to an even more disastrous event. Tied together, Alpine-style, the men were making their way down the mountain when Simpson slid and fell off a cliff. Still tied together, the hikers were fifty feet apart. Yates could not hear Simpson's yells over the wind, but he felt the weight of his partner's body and went through every possible scenario in his head to try to save Simpson. In the end, with hypothermia setting in, he knew the only thing he could do was cut the rope. He was sure his friend was dead from the fall or from exposure by now.

But Simpson was not dead. He plummeted the rest of the way down, landing in a thirty-foot crevasse. In his book *Touching the Void*, he writes that he could have easily given up then. But thinking about dying there, all alone, was unbearable. A "sickening sense of loneliness" overcame him, and it was what kept him going. He crawled on his stomach through the crevasse until he saw light at the end, and he finally made it out. From there he had a six-mile hike to base camp, a distance that seemed overwhelming. "And then it occurred to me that maybe I should set definite targets. I started to look at things and think right, if I can get over to that crevasse over there in 20 minutes, that's what I'm going to do . . . If I got there in 22 or 24 minutes, I was upset almost to the point of tears. It became obsessive. I think I knew the big picture was so big I couldn't deal with it." He hopped and crawled more than five miles. "Once I decided I was going to get to the rock in 20 minutes, I was going to bloody well do it. And it would help me, because I would get halfway through the distance and I would be in such pain that I couldn't bear the thought of getting up and falling again, but then I'd look at the time and think, 'I've got to get there.' It seemed like there was a very cold, pragmatic part of me that was saying you have to do this, this and this if you're going to get there. It was quite insistent."[2] Eventually he made it back to base camp, and Simpson and Yates made it back home, together.

Simpson clearly used his mental strength to overcome the physical hardships he was facing. And it was through setting attainable, measurable, and realistic goals that he was able to reach the final goal of making it safely back to base camp.[3]

5

ADAPTIVE THINKING

"**G**ET YOUR HEAD IN** the game!" How many times have you heard this yelled to players making stupid mistakes? You might even say it to yourself before tackling a big project. We hear this saying all the time; most of us know it means to focus on the activity at hand. But did you ever take time to think about the actual words? Getting your head in the game is not something to be taken lightly. Being able to focus and be in a positive mental state are crucial for peak performance.

So the question is, how do you do it? The solution is relatively simple but probably not something you want to hear: Truly getting your head in the game is hard work. You must apply the same discipline, time, and resources to being mentally prepared that you do physically in any sort of game, whether on the field, in the boardroom, or out on the battlefield.

"Get your head in the game" is more than just a saying used to encourage athletes. There is a concept in psychology commonly referred to as the thought–performance relationship. This means our performance is heavily influenced by our thoughts. Our thoughts evoke certain emotions, which then trigger a physiological response that directly affects what we do and how we perform. This sequence can go either well or badly, depending on the thought. For example, a negative thought such as "There's no way I can get this job; I'm underqualified" could evoke an emotion like fear or frustration, which then makes you nervous and you flub the interview. On the other hand, a positive thought such as "I'm going to ace this test" can give you the confidence you need to excel.

Our thoughts instantly create a picture in our mind and evoke not only emotions but also memories. People carry around images about themselves in their subconscious, all of which are a part of who they are and how they perform. These "pictures" begin at birth and continue throughout life, capturing all our experiences and filing them away. These experiences reflect both the successes and failures in our lives. The manner in which they are interpreted helps your brain store them in either a negative memory slot or a positive memory slot.

If you ask people to recall their earliest memory, you will usually find that it is a negative one: a humiliation, a scary moment, or a big disappointment. The focus on a fear-inducing event makes evolutionary sense. If you are a caveman who knows that saber-toothed tigers hunt during a certain time because you came across one hunting first thing in the morning and it scared the life out of you, you remember not to go hunting at that time of day and it will help you live longer.

But how does remembering that you got a D in physics or that you humiliated yourself in front of your fifth-grade crush help you to survive? Unfortunately, we are programmed to have more negative thoughts about ourselves, our place in the world, and our daily lives. Rather than saving our lives, these thoughts undermine our performance abilities.

If an image that you pull up in a performance situation is what you do not want to happen, it will happen because you make it so. If you are a golfer and approach a hole with a water hazard in front, you might think, "Don't hit the water." But in thinking that, your mind creates a picture of your ball hitting the water. Your mind does not include the "don't" part of that sentence; it just illustrates the ball going into the water, and then that is what you end up thinking.

How do you change the outcome? The solution is to change the way we think.

We all talk to ourselves. But what are we saying? Whatever self-talk phrases we have, whether they are positive or negative, when they are repeated over and over again (like a closed loop), they become self-fulfilling prophesies. Whatever you are thinking becomes reality, because your expectations drive it to happen. It is the way the brain works. It will take your thoughts and turn them into actions, making what you are thinking become true, like a prophet whose visions become reality. So whatever you "feed" your brain the most will end up being what you do the most, positive or negative.

CONTROLLING THE NEGATIVE VOICES
IN OUR HEADS

Negative thoughts in our lives have the potential to lead to pessimism. Pessimism can lead to helplessness or hopelessness, helplessness can lead to depression, and depression can lead to suicide.

What is interesting is that as a society, the only time we intervene in the process is when a person gets clinically depressed. Then psychologists and psychiatrists will start on behavioral therapy or prescribe medication to mask symptoms. But if we backtrack and start with the negative thinking and intervene then, we can stop it from ever getting to that point.

Given the negativism surrounding so many people's lives, being positive and having trust and confidence in your ability is really hard work. Luckily, you can retool your thought process and not think about that ball going in the water, not think about the other people who are up for the job you apply for. You can have more control over your thoughts.

One of the first parts of this process is to become *aware* of your thoughts. Your mind has a constant narrative running about your day. As you sit at your computer at work, your brain may be thinking, "Gee, I'm really tired. My back hurts. When should I get lunch? Should I get another cup of coffee first? Ugh, I really don't want to have that conference call with Bill at one. My day would be so much easier if I didn't have to talk to him. Now, where are those numbers again that I need?" You may think these thoughts are all due to your circumstances, but they are not. You do have control.

It has been estimated that up to 80 percent of the thoughts we have in any given day (estimated in the vicinity of fifty thousand thoughts per day) are negative. The reason for this could be because of our primal instincts to survive. As humans evolved over time, everything was a threat, so we always had to consider the risk of what we were doing. But in this day and age, unless you live in a war zone, there are very few things that are threatening. Yet we still have the negative thoughts and still feel overwhelmed by our prospects in life.

For instance, think of how many people fear flying when statistically flying is far safer than driving. But even knowing the fear is illogical, our brains still feel that being in a tin can thirty thousand feet up in the air is a dangerous thing.

Think of the fear of sharks. Even though very few people die as a result of shark bites, the fear of sharks keeps many people out of the oceans.

There are other kinds of negative thoughts, everyday thoughts about ordinary things like bills, traffic, housework, chores, kids, bosses, and coworkers. These negative thoughts pile up on one another, clouding our days, so that they overwhelm us with negativity, and the things that get us happy and excited tend to get lost in the shuffle.

We have to be more in control over what we think. It affects everything in our lives, and not just our ability to perform in stressful situations. Think of negative thoughts as that major distraction that keeps us from doing well and succeeding in life.

The first step in controlling your thoughts and getting rid of negativity is to become aware of what you are thinking in the first place. Become an observer in your own life. Set the alarm on your phone for a few times during the day. When it goes off, stop and see if you can remember what you have been thinking about for the past few minutes. Write it down. This exercise helps you become more aware.

I knew a woman who was overwhelmed by negative thoughts every time she pulled into the parking lot of her local grocery store. She thought about what terrible parkers people were, how people took forever to get into and out of parking spaces, and how people could not be bothered to put away their carts properly. This negative stream of consciousness played out in her head while she was shopping, and she was always in a terrible mood by the time she got back home to her kids. Once she realized where her thoughts were going, though, she made it a priority to turn off that negative tape that was playing in her head and try to have positive thoughts instead. For instance, she might look at a new car model and admire it, enjoy the fact that the sun was out after a string of rainy days, or think about how lucky she was to be able to afford and easily access the healthy food she was about to buy.

When you become aware of a negative thought, focus on stopping that thought dead in its tracks. When the brain has a gap or a void, then it typically has a tendency to fill the gap. The next step in the process of learning to change your thinking is to fill the gap with something positive. It is so important to be intentional with our attention. Say you are in a situation where you think something like, "This day is going terribly. I've got so much to do, and none of it is going right." Stop that thought process! Shift it into something like, "I'm alive. I'm breathing. I can move and walk. I can come and go as I please." Point out your capabilities as opposed to your inabilities.

Once you begin practicing control of your thoughts, it will become second nature. As you find errant thoughts entering your head ("I hope I don't fail this test"; "I'm terrible at public speaking"; "My hair never looks good"), take these steps:

1. *Concentrate* on the thought for a moment.
2. Say, *"Stop"* to yourself.
3. *Replace* the negative thought with a positive counter-thought.

The trick (and this is crucial) is to have a positive, effective thought ready at hand, or else your mind will go back to your original thought. You can develop these ready-made thoughts by becoming aware of what you are thinking in these situations. Create real counter-thoughts and then practice the switch on a regular basis. You must make this automatic if you expect to use it in a performance situation. Repetition is all you need. Remember, the brain learns through repetition. Repeat the right thoughts for the right performance occasions, and they become automatic, just like your negative thoughts have.

For instance, the veterans we work with may wake up in pain from their injuries. It might be easy for them to think, "I'm not doing well today," and want to just sit on the couch to avoid exacerbating their pain. Instead, they have to hype themselves up to be mobile. "I feel good today. I'm going to get up and get out, and take on the world and accomplish what I need to accomplish."

When you set your mindset to adaptive thinking, your outlook will start to change. "Today is going to be a good day. No matter what happens throughout this day, it's going to be a good day." If somebody steals your parking spot, brush it off, stop the negative thoughts, and keep the dialogue positive. So often somebody can say something that triggers a frustrating response: doctors who do not understand, a spouse, a credit card company. Realize that it is just a moment: "This is small. I have no need to be frustrated. I can interact with these people and be more neutral." Positivity breeds positivity; negativity breeds negativity.

When creating your counter-thoughts, use statements that will motivate and empower you. These statements will reinvigorate you to push forward with your day-to-day plans.

IT IS ALL ABOUT CONFIDENCE

Let's look at confidence for a moment. Confidence is at the heart of all successful performances. But there are a lot of misconceptions surrounding confidence. Some people think you have to be born with a lot of it; or that loud, cocky, arrogant attitudes show confidence; or that you must first succeed to be confident. None of these are true. Of course, being successful helps boost confidence, but what about the times when you are involved in something where a clear signal of success comes much later? What keeps you going? This is where you apply positive, effective thinking. This is where you make self-talk work for you.

Confidence comes from within. Do not look for it from other people. Confidence cannot be given to you. It can be influenced, but it cannot be acquired from anyone else. How you think about what is happening is actually more important than what is happening. If you think you can, you can. If you do not, you will not. (Remember the Little Engine That Could, who said, "I think I can, I think I can," to make it up the mountain?) The reason is that our response to any event will be primarily based on our interpretation of the event, not the event itself. Remember, your mind is racing at an incredible speed.

Henry Ford said, "If you think you can, or you think you can't, you're going to be right."[1] You're going to want to get the path to the desired result.

Take charge of that little voice in your head and make it work for you.

ADAPTIVE THINKING AT WORK

When you know you are going to have a performance event, such as a test, an interview, a game, or a contest, you need a preperformance routine to get your mind into a state where it can stay focused and "in the game." This involves what you do and think one hour before, thirty minutes before, and five minutes before the event. This ensures you are mentally prepared for the event.

An important part of a preperformance routine is setting up a specific cue, one that helps direct your focus toward the task at hand.

For example, here is a preperformance routine for someone with test anxiety.

One hour before, allow time to get focused. Work on your breathing strategies. Then look over your review sheet for your exam to get your mind into an academic mode.

Five minutes before, clear your mind, calm your mind, and relax your body.

When the test comes, know that if a question comes up that you do not recognize the answer to immediately, instead of viewing that negatively, move on to the next one, or put the test down, and focus on your breathing to calm down. Then pick your pencil back up and start where you left off.

When a veteran in the Apex Peak Performance Training program used that routine to take a test, the calm state he was in meant that his whole wealth of knowledge opened up, and he got an A. Previously, he would have been too anxious to take the test, envisioning failure and a bunch of questions that were too difficult, and gotten out of the testing room as quickly as possible in a fight-or-flight reaction. Here, when that anxiety reaction kicked in, he knew he had to regain his composure. With the help of breathing techniques, positive self-talk, and imagery, his results were great.

Adaptive thinking does not end with your performance. To improve, you need to take time after the event to evaluate the situation and how you did. It is extremely important not to criticize yourself in the negative. Do not think: You are an idiot for doing that, saying that, or thinking that. Find a way to appreciate the performance, and say things like, "I did the best that I could. I'll see what the results are. I feel great with what I did, and now I'll move on with my plans for the rest of the day." You need to file the memory of that performance event in the positive column in your brain.

Here are some further tips:

- Play to your strengths. What are your good features? Think about them often, and leverage them for confidence.
- Seek the company of positive individuals. If you are hanging out with folks who are negative, you might consider hanging out with more positive people.

- Surround yourself with inspirational material. It really does work. The brain takes it all in and, through repetition, makes it permanent.
- When faced with setbacks, focus on what you can do to get back in the game.

The one thing in life you have total control over is what you are thinking. Make it work for you.

6

STRESS AND ENERGY MANAGEMENT

THE WORD *STRESS IS* used to describe a wide variety of situations, from the seemingly small stress of being unable to reach someone on her cell phone to the feelings associated with having too much work and not enough time to the extreme stress of the death of a loved one. One of the more widely accepted definitions is by Richard S. Lazarus: "Stress is a condition experienced when a person perceives that demands exceed the personal and social resources the individual is able to mobilize."[1] In other words, the term is used to describe our *response* to an event based on how we perceive the event and not the event itself. We especially feel stressed when we feel that things are out of control.

Our perception of our ability to cope or even thrive with the demands placed on us is fundamental to our experience of stress. For example, moving to start a new job for which you are well prepared might be a wholly exciting experience. If, however, starting that job comes at the same time that one of your children is about to enter his senior year in high school where you are presently located, you might feel conflicted, making it hard to decide what to do.

We can feel stress when faced with choices in life, but we can also feel stressed when placed in certain situations, even if that place is where we wanted to be. My four years at West Point were a very stressful time for me. It was an environment that placed demands on us each and every day, academically, physically, and mentally. I knew that to thrive at West Point, not just survive, I would have to adapt and manage the stress. I became self-disciplined, motivated, focused, and driven. Those four years became the foundation for everything I did after graduation, shaping my personality and also laying the groundwork for the research I would do on mental agility and control.

Stress comes from demanding or unexpected events in our lives, but not all are equally difficult. One element of a good stress management program is having the ability to measure your current stress level based on the events in your life. Knowing where you are with respect to stress at any given moment provides you with the opportunity for more precise and effective stress management intervention.

The Holmes-Rahe Social Readjustment Rating Scale, commonly referred to as the Holmes-Rahe Stress Scale, was designed to do just that in a standardized and reliable way.[2] This instrument helps measure the day-to-day stress load we carry, or what I call "walk-around stress." It is the stress you feel every day as a result of events that have happened to you over a period of time and that dissipates only with the passage of time. Knowing where you are goes a long way in helping you decide what to do to manage the stress in your life.

HOLMES-RAHE SOCIAL READJUSTMENT RATING SCALE[3]

Indicate which of the following events have happened to you within the past twelve months by circling the value associated with that event. If the event has occurred more than once, add the value indicated the number of times the event has occurred. (For example, if you have had a change in residence twice, which has a value of 20, you would double it and then give yourself a score of 40 for that item.)

LIFE EVENT	VALUE
Death of spouse	100
Divorce	73
Marital separation	65
Jail term	63
Death of close family member	63
Personal injury or illness	53
Marriage	50
Fired at work	47
Marital reconciliation	45
Retirement	45
Change in health of family member	44
Pregnancy	40
Sex difficulties	39
Gain of new family member	39
Business adjustment	39
Change in financial state	38

Death of a close friend	37
Change to different line of work	36
Change in number of arguments with spouse	35
Mortgage over $300,000	31
Foreclosure of mortgage or loan	30
Change in responsibilities at work	29
Son or daughter leaving home	29
Trouble with in-laws	29
Outstanding personal achievement	28
Spouse begins or stops work	26
Begin or end school	26
Change in living conditions	25
Revision of personal habits	24
Trouble with boss	23
Change in work hours or conditions	20
Change in residence	20
Change in schools	20
Change in recreation	19
Change in church activities	19
Change in social activities	18
Mortgage or loan less than $300,000	17
Change in sleeping habits	16
Change in number of family get-togethers	15
Change in eating habits	15
Vacation	13

Christmas   12

Minor violations of the law   11

TOTAL = _____

Scores on the Holmes-Rahe Stress Scale indicate the following:

300+ You have a high or very high risk of becoming ill in the near future.

150–299 You have a moderate chance of becoming ill in the near future.

< 150 You have only a low to moderate risk of becoming ill in the near future.

A primary reason for the relationship between levels of stress and susceptibility to illness is that stress, especially from anxiety or worry, compromises the immune system, making you more vulnerable to illness and infection. The greater the stress, the greater the likelihood of getting sick.

It is also important to recognize what stress is and what it is *not*. The word *stress* is quite often misused, seen as both cause and effect. First, the word *stress* does not refer to a causing event, but to a response to that event. Stress is a nonspecific response to an event that is perceived as demanding or threatening. That means that a stressor (cause) inherently has neither positive nor negative valence, but is determined largely by the perceptions of the individual. Even "good" events can be stressful. For example, a wedding or a vacation can be just as stressful for some as the threat of losing a job. When considering stress, we must think of two simultaneous events, an external event called the *stressor*, and the mental, emotional, and physiological *responses* associated with that event.

The Chinese have recognized stress as both positive and negative for centuries. The Chinese symbol for stress is 应力 and is translated into *danger* and *opportunity*. It suggests a double-edged sword that cuts both ways—there can be a benefit as well as a cost. In the Western world, we tend to address stress primarily as a negative factor, a bad thing. When it is large and unremitting, it certainly can be. But the Chinese description suggests that there is a beneficial side to stress, and that it can be useful as well as harmful. This is a much broader and more useful way to look at stress. Taken in this broader context, the psychophysiological components of stress turn out to be something we actually need to survive and even thrive as human beings, up to a point. For example, the resources we need to either engage or avoid a threat are automatically triggered by the autonomic nervous system. The body responds with involuntary functions such as increased heart rate, rapid breathing to gain more oxygen, muscles tensing for action, narrowing of attention, and so on.

Later in this chapter, I describe this autonomic nervous system response, better known as the *fight-or-flight* response, and the relationship between stress and performance. That relationship is curvilinear, and it shows that some level of stress is actually helpful because it activates body systems that are critical for responding to and acting on external events. In this chapter, I want to emphasize that stress can be helpful as well as harmful and show that the beneficial effects of stress can be achieved by understanding the mechanisms that trigger the stress response, and the voluntary actions you can initiate to moderate and manage that response.

How much of a problem is stress? It is substantial, especially when it is unremitting. A number of studies have indicated the following:

- 75 to 90 percent of all doctor visits in the United States are for stress-related disorders.
- 80 percent of all disease and illness in the United States is initiated or aggravated by stress.
- Eight out of ten of the top ten prescription drugs are given for stress-related disorders.
- The number of workers indicating they are feeling highly stressed has doubled since 1985.
- According to the American Institute for Stress, the effects of stress cost American businesses $300 billion a year. This total includes ever-increasing healthcare costs, accidents, absenteeism, employee turnover, and reduced productivity.

Job stress has become the twenty-first-century disease and is considered a global epidemic.[4]

Each year, stress-related healthcare costs are a large chunk of overall business costs.[5] Work-related stress factors include being overloaded with responsibilities and meeting tough deadlines, feeling rushed to finish projects, and communication problems with coworkers. As stress increases, we become more and more irritable and increasingly more short-tempered with others. Many people feel unappreciated for their efforts and thus develop a "What's the point?" attitude.

Can we identify key business forces that contribute to workers feeling stressed? The answer is a resounding yes. For example, because of technology and workers being seemingly available 24-7, it becomes extremely difficult to clearly separate work and home life. Not to mention because of frequent mergers and acquisitions, there is little job security anymore. Figure 6.1 summarizes the work environment and its direct impact on the ability of today's workforce to perform at the levels needed for companies to be competitive.

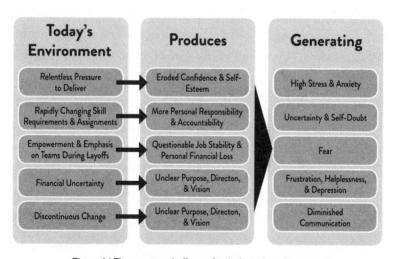

Figure 6.1 The causes and effects of today's work environment.

The relentless pressure to deliver quality products and services cuts across every business organization. Such a climate can lead to employee burnout and the feeling of being overwhelmed. Downsizing the workforce while at the same time not adjusting the work demands on the "survivors" is a major contributor to this. Doing more with less has become the new normal.

With downsizings and restructurings, employees also face changing skill requirements and job assignments for which they often have little or no training or qualifications. In time, working under such conditions erodes a person's confidence and self-esteem. Lack of confidence can make people hesitant and risk averse. Under high pressure and stress conditions, such hesitancy can become paralysis, and risk aversion becomes avoidance.

As companies moved strongly toward more empowerment and emphasis on teams, business results showed significant improvements in productivity and employee satisfaction. However, there were also casualties and unintended consequences. Many employees who were excellent individual contributors quickly discovered that they were uncomfortable and stressed in a team environment. One of the hallmarks of a close-knit, highly effective team is a sense of accountability and responsibility, not only for one's own contribution and welfare but also for that of other team members. For individuals with a strong sense of accountability and responsibility for their own work but a discomfort with assuming that for others, being part of a team can be quite stressful.

One of the greatest concerns and a constantly looming stressor for employees is work–life balance. The ability to enjoy the fruits of our labor as well as family and friends is vital to the motivation and morale of today's workforce. The delicate work–life balance is being threatened now more than ever. The transformation of work through information and communication technology is a major contributor to the blurred lines between when we work and when we play. What initially started as "anytime, anywhere" has become "all the time, everywhere." The resultant job instability and uncertainty over the proper work–life balance threatens our health and wellness.

Stress management can provide the self-control and self-mastery training that allows people to reduce the effects of stress and therefore reduce illness, sick day rates, and medical attention costs, while substantially increasing performance and productivity. We need to learn to deal with these stressors in a much more effective and efficient way. We do this to not only cope with adversity but to actually thrive in it.

What is the underlying culprit behind our stress response? It is an evolutionary mechanism called the autonomic fight-or-flight response,[6] which triggers powerful mental, emotional, and physiological responses to threatening events. It goes back to prehistoric times, when the primary threats to our ancestors were physical ones, whether wild animals or unfriendly rival tribes. In such threats of physical harm, our ancestors had to possess the ability to quickly respond physically in order to either fight or flee from the danger. Either way, instant activation of automatic bio-systems was needed.

When confronted with a threat, the fight-or-flight trigger suddenly activates the adrenal glands and increased hormone secretion such as norepinephrine and cortisol, resulting in increased heart rate, muscle tone, blood flow, breathing rate, and so on. The sudden flow of psychophysiological resources through sympathetic nervous system activation provided our ancestors the chance to survive the physical threat. Once the threat was gone, another part of our autonomic nervous system, the *parasympathetic system*, kicked in to bring everything back to a normal, balanced level, reducing our heart rate, decreasing our blood pressure, slowing down our breathing, relaxing the muscles, and generally just calming us down.

The problem today is more complicated. Given the development of our thinking and imagining brain, this same primitive response mechanism kicks in even for threats that are not physically derived but are imagined. And so our sympathetic nervous system fires with all the same physiological responses, even though it is not a physical fight-or-flight situation. Unable to fight or flee, we experience a constant level of system activation that, over time, can have deleterious health consequences. Figure 6.2 lists the common changes associated with stress.[7]

As you can see, stress affects our most fundamental functions needed to survive and thrive as humans. Learning to control and regulate the underlying cause of these effects is a key step toward enhancing performance and improving health and wellness.

PHYSIOLOGICAL	MENTAL	BEHAVIORAL
• Increased heart rate and blood pressure • Increased sweating • Increased pupil dilatation • Rapid respiration • Increased blood flow to skin • Increased muscle tension • Increased oxygen intake • Increased blood sugar levels • Cotton mouth	• Worry • Feeling overwhelmed • Unable to decide • Feeling confused • Loss of concentration • Unable to direct attention • Feeling not in control • Narrowing of attention	• Rapid talking • Nail biting • Foot tapping • Muscle twitching • Pacing • Scowling • Increased blinking • Yawning • Trembling • Broken voice

Figure 6.2 Common issues associated with stress.

Now that you have a better understanding of what stress is and what it is not, let's look at the relationship between stress and performance, and strategies for managing stress so it can serve as a driving force for enhanced performance.

PERFORMANCE STATES: THE RELATIONSHIP BETWEEN STRESS AND PERFORMANCE

Until recently, the conventional wisdom on how stress and performance were related suggested a linear relationship. With that in mind, much of the training in athletics and the military was driven by the idea that the more stress you created in training, the greater the performance. It was based on the idea that adding pressure and stress to practice situations would "toughen" individuals and there-fore make them better performers.

For example, the training of U.S. Army Rangers and Navy SEALs has always involved pushing soldiers to the limit to prepare them for the rigors of their specific type of combat. Making training tough and pushing to the limit does result in better performance, but at what price? Many learn to sur-vive and make it through successfully. The essential issue with that kind of model is that it has a high failure rate. Even people who are selected and are highly qualified to engage in this kind of program fail. The failure rate from the Navy SEALs BUD/S (Basic Underwater Demolition/SEAL) train-ing program is about 80 percent. This is the Navy SEALs' basic entry-level training that accepts qualified recruits but then pushes them through the most rigorous mental, emo-tional, and physical training in the military.[8]

In their classic inverted-U curve, Robert Yerkes and John Dillingham Dodson showed the relationship between arousal and performance to be a curvilinear one.[9] *Arousal* is generally defined as activation of autonomic nervous system responses to threatening or potentially harmful events. Their finding provides a more accurate and research-based framework for describing the relationship between arousal and performance. Their research suggests that a certain amount of initial activation and arousal is actually good for you, but too much is harmful. By substituting *stress* for *arousal*, we can use their general finding as a way to portray the rela-tionship between stress and performance. We can also view the relationship as having three general performance states.

Figure 6.3 shows that initially an increase in stress is actually beneficial in becoming activated. But with continued stress and being overly activated, performance will suffer as the various automatic responses to the stress continue to kick in. The figure shows that there is an optimal stress level that results in the best performance, commonly referred to as the area of peak performance or optimal performance.

In the early stages when there is not enough stress, performance is low because there is little activation, little physiological arousal. This is the situation where some stress is needed to move up the curve to improve performance and where motivation can play a role in getting there. Once you increase stress by allowing yourself to feel some anxiety or nervousness or concern for doing well, you actually trigger just the right amount of sympathetic activity to

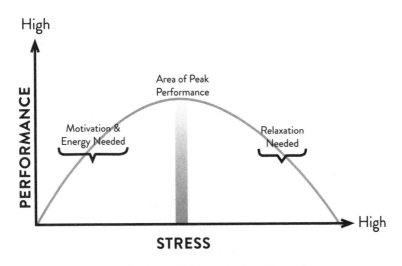

Figure 6.3 The relationship between performance and stress.

increase alertness and overall physical and cognitive functioning. This improves performance and moves you toward the middle on the stress–performance curve. This is the energy and activation level that athletes often describe as being in "the zone" or "peak performance." Here, relative calm, focus, alertness, and emotional self-control describe the mental, emotional, and physiological state of the athlete.

However, if the stress continues unmitigated, performance deteriorates. Now you would find yourself overly activated, overly anxious, or even fearful, and the fight-or-flight response is in full gear. You find it difficult to focus, to be clearheaded, to make sound decisions, to plan, to perform. Once you are in this performance state, you need ways to calm yourself quickly, to regain composure and control. You need techniques that counterbalance the activation of the sympathetic nervous system and produce a homeostasis that allows you to bring to bear all your skills and abilities to perform at your best. The remaining sections of this chapter detail techniques that give you control over your stress responses and bring a recovery essential for performing in pressure and stress situations.

It is important to realize that the curvilinear relationship is not fixed; it varies from person to person. In other words, the height (level of performance) and width (level of stress) of the curve will vary, depending on your developmental experiences, personality, formal mental skills training, exposure to and coping with stressful situations in the past, and a positive, supportive environment versus a negative, unsupportive one. Whatever your developmental experiences, it will always be curvilinear. Everyone experiences the three performance states, just in different magnitudes.

Being keenly aware of what you are thinking, what you are feeling, and how you are responding physiologically is essential for performing at your best when it matters most. Managing stress and energy involves constant monitoring of your emotional and physiological responses to events and possessing the prerequisite mental skills for regaining control and performing at the levels to which you have trained and worked so hard.

If we intervene at the very first part of this process, that is, the environment, we call it environmental engineering. If possible, this should be the first intervention. If you can change the environment, then the other parts of the process change as well. For example, when you walk into a dentist's office and soft, soothing music is playing, it is an attempt to engineer the environment to be less stressful. Unfortunately, more often than not, the ability to change what is happening is not an option. Most of the time, we have little control over the outside world and can rarely change external events.

So the first place you can directly intervene in this sequence is in your thinking. In Chapter 5, you learned a number of techniques for determining and changing your thoughts: thought stopping, thought replacement, rational thinking, and self-talk management. In this chapter, more emphasis is placed on the emotion part of this relationship and its impact on both physiology and thoughts. Emotion plays a role in activating the sympathetic nervous system and thus the resultant physiological responses.

TRIGGERING THE RELAXATION RESPONSE

The most commonly known techniques for countering the fight-or-flight response fall into the category of relaxation exercises. It has been known for some time now that the mind and body are inextricably linked; each influences the other. You cannot relax without the mind, and you cannot relax without the body. The history of relaxation dates back more than twenty-five hundred years. Yoga, perhaps the earliest form of "relaxation," can be traced back to India more than five thousand years ago.

The modern history of relaxation begins in the 1920s with Edmund Jacobson, who developed a technique called progressive relaxation, in which patients were taught to progressively relax their muscles. Dr. Jacobson's premise was that relaxing the muscles of the body would make a person feel more relaxed in general. In the 1960s, Hans Selye, an endocrinologist, was the first to document the consequences of stress on the immune system. He introduced the three phases of the stress response—alarm, resistance, and exhaustion—in his general adaptation syndrome. Dr. Selye also coined the word *stressor*, which since has become a part of the stress vocabulary.[10]

Around the same time, Dr. Herbert Benson, a cardiologist at Harvard, was studying the medical benefits of relaxation. He proved beyond any doubt that the mind–body connection did in fact exist. He demonstrated that simple relaxation techniques could lower people's blood pressure, slow their heart rates, and calm their brain waves. He called the effect "the relaxation response" and popularized it in his 1975 book, *The Relaxation Response.* Here are some of the most documented benefits of using relaxation techniques:

- Reduce the risk of heart disease by 30 percent
- Significantly reduce the risk of high blood pressure, heart attacks, and fatal heart attacks
- Reduce the risk of a depression recurrence by 50 percent
- Help treat anxiety and panic attacks.
- Strengthen the immune system.[11]

The most commonly used relaxation exercises/techniques follow. When selecting which one(s) you should use, consider the following factors: How comfortable are you with the exercise? How effective is the exercise in producing relaxation for you? How much time do you have available to engage in the exercise?

RHYTHMIC BREATHING

Rhythmic breathing involves becoming aware of your breath and deliberately changing the timing of your inhales and exhales. A paced breathing exercise serves two major purposes within the context of our program. First, focused breathing using the diaphragm (the muscle that controls the expansion and contraction of our lungs) stimulates major nerves in our parasympathetic nervous system, which is responsible for balancing out our stress response.[12] Additionally, breathing can be done anywhere, and it is something everyone has been doing for their entire lives. It does not require equipment or much time at all, and paced breathing can be taught in seconds. We typically instruct our clients to place a hand on the stomach just below the rib cage and inhale through the nose for about four seconds while feeling the stomach expand. This is followed by a six-second exhale while feeling the stomach compress and get pulled toward the spine. This exercise is perfect for those just starting a stress management program because it often shows noticeable results within minutes, if not seconds.

MEDITATION

Meditation involves focusing your attention in such a way that you feel calm and gain a deeper awareness of yourself. Eastern philosophies have recognized the health benefits of meditation for thousands of years, and only more recently has it found its way into Western practice. The two meditation techniques most commonly used are concentrative, which focuses on a single image, sound, mantra, or your own breathing, and mindfulness, which emphasizes awareness of all thoughts, feelings, sounds, or images that pass through your mind at the time. Meditation involves sitting quietly for at least ten to fifteen minutes, accompanied by slow, rhythmic breathing. More often than not, the time frame is usually much longer.

PROGRESSIVE MUSCLE RELAXATION

Developed by Edmund Jacobson in the early 1920s,[13] progressive muscle relaxation is a technique for learning to gain awareness and control the state of tension of a particular muscle group (since the body responds to stress with tension). A relaxation session might consist of a full-body scan (checking in with your muscles) or modified by using specific muscle groups as you sit in a quiet room and comfortable chair. The objective is to focus on each muscle and then attempt to change the tension by deliberately tensing and relaxing each body area. Make sure you do not tense to such an extreme that it causes pain due to muscle cramping. You can add deep breathing by breathing in as you contract the muscles and relaxing them as you breathe out. You will feel the difference between tense and relaxed states. Also, actively engaging the muscle groups loosens and relaxes them. This particular relaxation technique is especially effective with athletes, who are very much in touch with the tense and relaxed state of their muscles. Progressive relaxation is especially popular with today's physical therapists. With the advent of smartphones, there are great relaxation and meditation apps available and easy to get.

AUTOGENIC RELAXATION

Autogenic training is a relaxation technique developed by the German psychiatrist Johannes Heinrich Schultz in 1932. In autogenic relaxation, the practitioner repeats a set of visualizations or imagery, usually related to warmth and heaviness, that induces a state of relaxation. This technique is used to influence your autonomic nervous system. Autogenic training restores the balance between the activity of the sympathetic (fight-or-flight) and the parasympathetic (rest-and-recover) branches of the autonomic nervous system.[14]

GUIDED IMAGERY RELAXATION

The brain does not differentiate between real and imagined experience; therefore, the body responds to both as though they were real. This principle helps make guided imagery a useful tool for relaxation since you usually imagine soothing, peaceful scenarios. Practitioners employ guided imagery to help clients using mental imagery, commonly referred to as visualization, to reduce stress. A typical session involves a script of a relaxing and calming scene that clients hear and then imagine in their minds. It is in some ways a form of self-hypnosis. A key advantage of guided imagery relaxation is that it involves all the senses, making the experience as real as possible.

BIOFEEDBACK

In recent years, as the technology and ease of use of its equipment became more prevalent, biofeedback as a relaxation technique has continued to grow. In its application, practitioners usually take the most basic elements of progressive and autogenic relaxation and develop simple versions that are used in conjunction with the biofeedback. Biofeedback relaxation is especially useful for people who have difficulty focusing inward and who struggle with self-awareness.

OUR USE OF BIOFEEDBACK

Biofeedback is a process by which we gain greater awareness of physiological functions, such as heart rate, breathing patterns, skin conductance, muscle tone, body surface temperature, and brain waves and their relation to stress. The goal of biofeedback training is to increase awareness, understand the physiological responses, and learn to manipulate them at will. Biofeedback technology and the accompanying instrumentation and equipment have seen a flurry of innovations and advancements in recent years. Equipment that used to be bulky, cumbersome, and not readily available has become streamlined, user-friendly with advanced sophistication, and readily available for qualified practitioners. Once relegated to the medical and clinical professions, biofeedback has seen a significant expansion as an effective training and feedback tool for enhancing performance. For example, for the 2010 Winter Olympics, Canada's goal for "owning the podium" was heavily driven and supported by sports psychologists utilizing sophisticated biofeedback equipment.[15]

We make extensive use of biofeedback as a training tool for developing the core mental skills of our clients. Trainers and coaches know the two fundamental requirements for learning a new skill are (1) a good knowledge and idea of what the skill looks like and (2) receiving good feedback as to progress in learning the skill. Mental skills are inner skills; in other words, they are inside as our thoughts, emotions, and physiological functions. As such, it is far more difficult to ascertain progress in developing these skills. This is where biofeedback comes in. Biofeedback can provide accurate and real-time feedback on the smallest of changes that might otherwise be imperceptible. As with any learning, even the smallest positive feedback is enough to provide the motivation to continue. I talk about how you can measure your performance matched with your stress release responses in Chapter 9.

Our training protocols start with a battery of standardized assessments along with a twelve-minute baseline biofeedback evaluation that measures physiological responses to a set of events that has been designed to evoke such responses. These assessments provide us with an accurate picture of the starting point for each individual. The biofeedback tools help accelerate and solidify the learning process. The ultimate goal of biofeedback training is to develop control and self-regulation of physiological responses to events in any situation without the use of any equipment.

RECOVERY FROM STRESS

It is unrealistic to believe that we could ever create a stress-free life. There are so many aspects of life that are threatening or difficult or challenging, all with the potential for inducing stress. In fact, some of the most satisfying and rewarding parts of our lives result from events and activities that are demanding and challenging, like winning a race or coming in first in a contest or creating something new. They give us a great sense of accomplishment. We like what we do; we enjoy the rewards and therefore persevere through potentially stressful situations. Stress management is not about trying to create stress-free situations, but about embracing potentially stressful challenges and demands to experience the joy of having done something that pushed you to the limits of your skills, knowledge, and abilities.

Because the fight-or-flight response kicks in automatically whenever we feel threatened, real or perceived, we need to have a more systematic way to acquire the necessary tools for controlling and regulating mental, emotional, and physiological responses to potentially stressful events. These stress management tools provide the means for recovery. Recovery ensures reengagement in the moment and continued high performance.

What are these recovery tools and techniques? Figure 6.4 portrays a balance between work–life stressors and counteracting recovery techniques. Note the various life events that can lead to stress. It is important to regard what impact each of these has and the stress it creates varies from person to person. In other words, whether or not you feel stress for any of these life events is strongly determined by factors like personality and experience.

STRESS	RECOVERY
• Life Stresses (Work/Home)	• Quantity/Consistency of Sleep
• Stress with Boss	• Quantity/Quality of R&R
• Extensive Travel	• Number of Small Meals
• Leadership Stressors	• Healthy Eating Habits
• Personal Expectations	• Regular Exercise
• Unforeseen Changes	• Proper Rest Periods
• Social Stressors	• Personal Time
• Health Stressors	• Fun Times
• Family Matters	• Relaxation Exercises

Figure 6.4 Stay Prepared and Maintain Balance.

Staying prepared is all about maintaining the balance between stress and recovery. Address stress by ensuring that extended periods of high-performance demands are balanced out with appropriate recovery. Recovery counterbalances daily stressors before they accumulate and become a significant impediment to performance. When you know an especially stress-filled period is approaching, plan and schedule recovery activities much like your work activity. Mark the recovery activities on the calendar, increasing the probability that you will engage in them.

Of all the recovery tools listed above, I want to focus on four of the most important: sleep, nutrition, exercise, and personal time. These are important not only because of the stress management resources they provide but also because they are tools that we as individuals can use and business organizations can provide. There is a direct relationship between how much stress time the body can handle and how much recovery time is needed. The more time devoted to recovery, the longer you can function in high-stress conditions with greater magnitude. Armed with this knowledge, organizations should be optimizing their work environments so that recovery tools are readily available and highly encouraged.

Unfortunately, too many organizations (businesses, military, sports, hospitals, education) do not pay enough attention to advocating or even reinforcing recovery activities, making it hard for people to routinely engage in them. With all the knowledge about stress and the idea of recovery, I find it difficult to understand the reluctance of organizations to incorporate meaningful and effective stress management activities. Some companies, however, have stepped up and taken dramatic steps for the betterment of their workers. One that comes to mind is Google. It created a work environment to keep its workers in the best mental, emotional, and physical shape with nap pods, relaxation rooms, cafeterias, basketball, allowing dogs to come to work, and so on.[16]

RECOVERY ACTIVITIES: SLEEP, EAT, EXERCISE, PERSONAL TIME

SLEEP

Perhaps no other recovery activity is as important as sleep. Not only does it have an effect on our physical wellness but it has a tremendous impact on our mental wellness, that is, brain health and function. More recent neuroscience discoveries demonstrate how critical sleep is to our well-being. Most of the important work of the brain in preparation for the next day is done while you are sleeping. Sorting, integrating, recalculating, and resetting are all critical functions accomplished during sleep. Interrupt sleep and you interrupt the completion of these critical functions. For example, we sleep in roughly ninety-minute cycles that have various stages, ranging from fully awake to deep sleep, or REM, to almost awake. We repeat these cycles throughout the night. Deep sleep is the most critical stage. It is here that our brains do their most critical work. If you awaken out of this stage, you feel tired, sluggish, and restless.

What are some of the things you can do to improve your sleep to gain the benefits of this important bodily function? Sleep is imperative for body and brain repair. We need about eight hours to fully restore ourselves, five to eight hours to maintain health, and we need to stay on a sleep routine.

Go to sleep and get up at the same time if you can only sleep a few hours. This helps provide a rhythm and to some extent can minimize waking from REM sleep.

Let us look at sleep versus the relaxation response. Is there a difference? Dr. Herbert Benson showed that triggering the relaxation response produces significantly less oxygen consumption than sleep. Triggering the relaxation response is not the same as sleeping in terms of the benefits and what is occurring within the body. During sleep, your oxygen consumption is higher because your body and brain are recovering from the day, and energy is needed to do this. But when engaging in relaxation, there is less oxygen consumption because the body is not working as hard, which enables true relaxation benefits for the body and nervous system and allows them to reach a more restful state.

Oxygen consumption is a measure of metabolism, among other factors, at any given moment, indicating the body at work with the sympathetic nervous system activated. Dr. Benson's research showed that triggering the relaxation response can produce a calming effect and can serve as an excellent supplement to sleep, especially if you have difficulties sleeping.

EAT

What you eat impacts both your mental and physical health. Never has paying attention to nutrition been more important than today. We consume way too much fast food, high sugars, high fats, carbohydrates, glutens, and so on. What we put in our bodies also affects our brains, and to a greater extent than we have realized. Neuroscience is demonstrating how beneficial certain foods are for the brain's health and proper functioning, and just how damaging some foods can be. Certain foods that have always been seen as especially beneficial for our bodies are now known to also boost brain health and functioning. For example, oatmeal settles nerves (stabilizes blood sugar); vitamin C in oranges decreases cortisol levels; bananas contain tryptophan, helping you sleep. Here are some tips that can keep you healthy and sharp, both physically and mentally.

- Choose healthy foods, especially brain healthy.
- Eat a balanced diet, incorporating all the major food groups.
- Drink plenty of water, sixty to eighty ounces a day.
- Consume four to six small meals throughout the day.
- Always plan your meals ahead of time, especially during those periods at work when you are so busy that you find yourself drifting to the snack machine because you are starving.

EXERCISE

We have always known the importance of exercise for our physical well-being, but only recently have we become aware of just how critical exercise is for the brain. For example, exercise stimulates the rate at which nerve cells bind to create new pathways, increasing the brain's storage capacity. Getting the body moving gets the mind moving, enhancing short-term memory, also known as working memory capacity. Here are just a few tips on exercising that can maximize the benefits you can gain from it, both physically and mentally.

- Exercising just thirty minutes most days of the week reduces the risk of chronic disease.
- You need sixty minutes of moderate to vigorous exercise at least three times a week to maintain your proper weight.
- Be sure to incorporate all three of these components into your exercise routine: cardio, stretching, and resistance. It is not enough just to run.

TIME-OUT

The one thing that suffers greatly in our busy and sometimes overwhelming lives is taking what I call a "time-out." Taking a time-out is one of the best ways to maintain balance, but it is most often left out. How often have you told yourself, "I have no time," "I'm too busy," or "I have too much to do"? Taking a time-out can be as short as a few minutes or as extended as a long-awaited vacation. Everyone can take a time-out. However, to have any chance that you will do it, you must plan for it, schedule it, and put it in your calendar every week. I do not know about you, but I live by my calendar. Typically, if it is not on my calendar, I end up not doing it. A good calendar should have not only work scheduled on it but also the other important things in your life. Those who indulge in activities they love are healthier, less depressed, and in better shape.[17] Here are some simple tips for taking your time-out.

- Listen to music. Music can produce calm energy and improved memory. Play the right kind of music, and you can achieve the right mind–body state.
- Talk with other people. We are social animals. We need the company of others. Interacting and socializing with other people is being neglected in today's wired lifestyle. Having 360 "likes" on Facebook is not the same as having 360 friends!
- Get outside; breathe some fresh air. Get away from your desk. Enjoy being outdoors, even if only for a few minutes. You would be amazed at how exhilarating a few deep breaths of fresh air can be.
- Do fun things (a hobby, sport, and so on). Time-out also means taking a little time just for yourself, doing the things that you enjoy. Do not lose the child within you.
- Get away from work at home and away from home at work.

RULES OF STRESS MANAGEMENT

RULE #1:

Know What You Can and Cannot Control

Ultimately the only thing you can *directly* control is what you think, say, and do. Trying to do otherwise will only lead to

STRESS AND ENERGY MANAGEMENT

frustration and much wasted effort and energy with little impact on improving performance. We delude ourselves into thinking and even wanting to control others. But you really cannot. People always have the choice of refusing to do what you want, even under threat of harm. Witness the countless martyrs throughout history who sacrificed their lives rather than give in to someone's attempts at control. Imagine how much better you could be if you were to put all your effort and energy into things over which you have control, rather than wasting them on what you cannot control.

RULE #2:

|||||||||||||||||||||||||||||||||||||||||||||||

Stress Is All About Perception and Reinterpreting

Our stress levels have much to do with how we perceive the events of the day. I reiterate here what I said earlier in Chapter 5: *It is not what happens to you that really matters, but how you think about what happens to you.* If you want to achieve your personal best, you must deliberately reinterpret your situation even to the point of embracing the stress response as somehow being *beneficial.* This is not about deceiving yourself or looking through rose-colored glasses. It is about looking for something potentially good in what is a bad situation. Put another way, this is the classic question: *Is the glass half-full or half-empty?* If something has the potential for energizing, you should view it in the best possible light so that what may be perceived as a threat can be seen as an opportunity instead. There is a wonderful line in the Oscar-winning film *The Sound of Music:* "When God closes a door, somewhere he opens a window." Give yourself a chance. Use self-talk to help.

The first thing that occurs after you perceive anything is you say something to yourself. You cannot help it. We are wired that way as part of our survival mechanism. But what comes to mind first is not what has to remain and affect your subsequent actions. Change the way you explain to yourself the *cause* of an event. Try to be factual and as accurate as possible. Above all, do not engage in catastrophic thinking, that is, making much more out of something than it really is, piling up negative thoughts, one on top of the other.

For example, imagine you have just left your boss's office after having been told the long-awaited report you have been preparing has not been done very well. Your thoughts and self-talk might go something like this:

> Wow! She didn't like my report. I worked so hard on it. I wonder which other of my reports she didn't like? I wonder if she thinks I'm not good at reports? I don't know—maybe I'm not? Wonder what else she thinks of me? Maybe I'm really not cut out for this job. Why did I ever get into this? She is going to fire me. I know she's going to fire me. I am going to lose my job, and then where will I be?

To ensure that you do not engage in catastrophic thinking, practice perpetual optimism. Watch the self-defeating thoughts. A doom-and-gloom outlook will only harm your ability to cope and, more important, thrive in a stress-filled situation. You always have a choice because by controlling your thoughts, you interpret what is happening.

RULE #3:

Stress Is Cumulative—a "Use It or Lose It" Plan for Recovery

As mentioned earlier, a certain amount of stress is actually beneficial. It allows for activation and arousal so that energy is gained for the moment. The right amount of stress and energy actually helps you focus sharper, think clearer, decide better, and perform at the level for which you have prepared yourself. The real harm from stress is when it is continuous and unmitigated. Unchecked, stress can be cumulative and damaging, not only to your performance but also to your health and wellness. You can manage your daily stress by *using* it as energy for exercising and *losing* it by engaging in relaxation exercises. Who hasn't felt better from exercise after a long, hard day, especially if it was also stress filled? The release of endorphins and other feel-good hormones dissipates the stress and gives temporary relief.

RULE #4:

Develop an Awareness of the Inevitable Parasympathetic Backlash

Powerful weariness and tiredness after long hours of work can occur even before we recognize it as affecting our performance. Another sign is that the mind wants to slow down in attention. Thinking patterns become less coordinated and logical, our memory is affected, and decision making becomes unreliable, confused—for example, putting groceries away in the wrong place, or forgetting to get off at your exit on the highway. This occurs when the parasympathetic system (the part of our nervous system that is there to bring us back to a balanced, calm, and collected state) overreacts as a result of prolonged activation of the sympathetic nervous system. In other words, in conditions of prolonged stress where our nervous system finally says *enough is enough,* the brain overreacts and, as a result, diminishes the effectiveness of many of the faculties needed to function at our best. You need to be aware of this and recognize the signs, especially in periods of high stress. A parasympathetic backlash rarely occurs for people who have mastered stress management techniques and are able to control their responses to various forms of stressors.

RULE #5:

Learn to Self-Regulate Through Relaxation and Physiological Control

This is about learning relaxation techniques that have been very effective in triggering the relaxation response. It is about training yourself to voluntarily control psychophysiological mechanisms that are fundamentally wired to be involuntary. Because you can learn to control these responses—heart rate, blood pressure, breathing, perspiration, surface temperature, and so on—lie detector tests are not admissible in court. Lie detectors measure the same physiological responses. Learning relaxation techniques gives you a counterbalance to sympathetic nervous system functions. As discussed earlier, the relaxation response is the trigger to the parasympathetic nervous system.

In summary, to be able to manage stress, we must organize stressors, focusing only on what we can control, make a deliberate commitment to practice optimism and adaptive thinking, reduce stress through exercise and relaxation exercises, balance heavy demands placed on us with appropriate amounts of recovery, and plan for recovery by putting it on our calendars just as we plan and schedule our other activities.

7

ATTENTION CONTROL

I N MOVIES LIKE *American Sniper*, the James Bond series, and Clint Eastwood's spaghetti Westerns, the entire focus of the movie is, for a few seconds, on the character getting ready to pull the trigger in an intense life-or-death situation. It is obvious in these situations that the person must erase all distractions and focus totally on the matter at hand. While most of us will never find ourselves in a situation where we have been asked to shoot someone, our days are filled with similar moments that require our complete attention.

The problem is, we are often distracted. Even when we want to pay attention, we cannot seem to get away from the millions of thoughts racing through our heads. And it is not just our own thoughts. The demand for our attention in modern society is unparalleled in both scope and intensity. We carry smartphones that alert us of news and events constantly, we are bombarded with news on Twitter, Facebook, and twenty-four-hour news channels, and we are constantly distracted by the "ping" of a notification of yet another text or email.

Yet the ways in which we learn to pay attention have not significantly changed in response to these new demands. We still primarily learn to attend to the right things at the right time through either trial-and-error experience or expert coaching. As new situations are encountered, we learn what information is useful and what is not; again, this is done through trial and error. This is a highly inefficient means for learning to pay attention, especially given today's demanding environment. The resultant attention deficit threatens to seriously cripple the workplace.

A radically new approach to addressing this attention challenge is needed. The Peak Performance Training program offered by Apex does exactly that, with attention control being one of the five parts of our process. This chapter presents a framework that helps explain the dimensions of attention and how to navigate through the model for maximizing attention efficiency and effectiveness. The combined use of a conceptual framework borrowed from sports psychology and the latest brain wave measurement technology has provided an opportunity to directly train individuals to significantly improve their attention control by focusing on *how* an individual pays attention and then learning to alter that in a highly efficient and effective way.

We know that it is incredibly easy to lose focus. The ability to zero in on just one thing at any one moment is actually hard work for the brain. The brain has a limited supply of resources available for the myriad functions it must carry out. In order to achieve maximum efficiency and effectiveness at any one moment, our brains borrow "energy" from other regions of itself that are not critical for the task at hand. Improving your attention control skills means training your brain to shut down the chatter in your head that comes from too much thinking about what you are doing.

ATTENTION RULE #1:

Right Before and Right After a "Shot," There Is No Thinking

Using sports psychology as a metaphor for performance situations, you cannot be effective in sports and allow your mind to shift from where it needs to be. Golfers should understand this more than anybody else, as golf is a game that is 90 percent mental. Even the great players lose concentration and react to distractions, internal or external, to the detriment of their putts or their drives off the tee.

Your thoughts interfere with the automatic body mechanisms you have worked so hard on in practice. If you think, you sink. Do all of your thinking when preparing for a shot you are about to make—what's the target, the distance, wind conditions, and so on. Once you are ready to take the shot, make sure it is silent in your brain.

ATTENTION RULE #2:

Our Attention Is Automatically Directed by the Brain's Orienting Response to External Stimuli

There are certain stimuli or events that automatically grab our attention—a loud noise, a cough, a sudden movement.

Our brains are conditioned to react to these events, and we shift our attention instantly.

According to the *Wall Street Journal,* office workers are interrupted—or self-interrupt—roughly every three minutes, and it can take up to twenty-three minutes to return to the original task. Incoming email, texts, phone calls, meetings, snacks in the break room—all of these can be a distraction from what a worker is there to do. Anyone in any situation can lose focus, even in the nonstressful home environment. For instance, have you gone into a room to retrieve something and forgotten what it was that you were there to do, and then got distracted by something else you saw that you wanted to do?

How can you deal with this natural tendency of our brains to be distracted by stimuli? You must completely immerse yourself in what you are doing at that moment, just as a child who is coloring a picture or playing with blocks can be completely absorbed in what he is doing. This takes deliberate practice, along with the recognition that you can be easily distracted. The trick is to avoid activities that interrupt the flow of the main task that needs your full attention. Stay in the present moment. If you know your phone is going to distract you, keep it turned off.

ATTENTION RULE #3:

It Is About Locking In, Not Blocking Out

How many times have we heard our colleagues say, "If only I could block out . . ."? People think that somehow they can train themselves to block out distractions when they need to. The bad news is that you cannot. The good news is you can eliminate distractions, just not in the way that you think.

If I ask you to block something out, where is your attention? It is on the very thing I am asking you to block out because I just directed your attention to it. For instance, if I said, "We're going to have a small birthday celebration in the conference room for Jay. Don't let it affect the fact that you have a deadline at noon, though." After that, you might be sitting in your office, with the news of the party running through your head, thinking about the cake you will eat later. The only thing you can do in this case is not "block" the thought of the party from your mind, but instead "lock" in on the task at hand, almost using the party as motivational energy to wrap up your work in time to relax and fully enjoy yourself at the celebration. Instead of spending your energy trying to say, "Don't think about the cake," say something like, "Let's knock out these sales calls!" Or, "Two more spreadsheets!"

ATTENTION RULE #4:

Under Pressure and Stress, Attention Automatically Narrows

Attention narrows so much that it becomes difficult to perform at your best because you are unable to take in all the relevant information you need to successfully perform the task. This automatic response goes back to prehistoric times, when the sudden narrowing of attention due to a threat was a survival mechanism. When a lion approached, it was no time to be admiring the beautiful leaves on a nearby tree or contemplating the colors of the sunrise. No, it was time to lock in on the lion. Unfortunately, this same response mechanism is still with us, even though most physical threats to humans no longer exist.

The brain does not distinguish between real and imagined threats. So when you feel the pressure and stress of a tight match in your league soccer tournament, your attention will narrow too much (to find that lion) and you will miss important information that you need to make a good shot. Take a deep breath and calm yourself; you will signal to your body and brain that this is not a time of danger, and your attention will broaden once again to focus on what is relevant and needed for that task.

ATTENTION RULE #5:

|||||||||||||||||||||||||||||||||||||||||||||||||||||||||||||||||||||||||||||||||||||||||||

Use a Solid Preperformance Routine

Routines keep you focused on the task at hand. They keep you from overthinking your performance. They aid you in emotional, physical, and mental preparation, and help redirect your focus when lost or distracted. They help maintain your focus and confidence.

Routines can also help direct our response to a place. We never know what dynamic we are going to be walking into, but having a routine will help you maintain attention control.

For instance, when we train clients to achieve in a performance situation, such as taking a test, we teach them it is important to focus on the test itself and not what is going on in front of them. Also focus on breathing: Have smooth, steady breaths in a consistent rhythm. There will be distractions, such as a person tapping his pencil, the sound of people turning their papers, and people walking back and forth to hand in their papers. All these things can make a person lose focus, which in turn might mean she loses the ability to tap into the knowledge she needs to complete the test, or she allows doubt or fear that she can do well to creep in. We help clients strategize to regain focus, to not give up, to take one question at a time.

In our brain-training rooms, we have our trainees take tests. We track them and then insert visual or auditory distractions. We have them quiet their thoughts, then take a test while being challenged.

We introduce blaring sounds, and they have to block out the sound and really amplify their attention to the task at hand, while allowing the sound to penetrate. They have to dial up their attention to stay engaged. We have studies showing how, with training, people can focus in on their task no matter what we throw at them.

There are many situations in everyday life where we need to practice attention control. And the effects of losing our attention can be devastating. For example: driving. Distracted driving has become a leading cause of car accidents in the United States, many resulting in death. Whether you are distracted by kids in the backseat, the radio, or your phone, taking your thoughts away from the activity at hand can be dangerous. People do not have enough practice in attention control to focus on what they need to be doing.

Other examples are writing a paper or a project for work. Something that should take you twenty minutes takes one to two hours, all because you lose focus and cannot maintain attention control.

A study by Eric Altman of Michigan State found that interruptions lasting just seconds managed to double the error rate for participants taking a test. The length of interruption does not matter—one second, one millisecond. Just the distraction itself was enough to affect performance.

Staying focused is the way to keep your head in the game. At Apex, we help you set goals and then give you the tools to achieve those goals. One way is through practicing our rules of attention, to heighten your sense of focus and enable your brain to learn to focus on one thing at a time. Remember, there is no multitasking. Instead, do one task successfully and then move on to the next. Once you have learned to focus, you will achieve your goals with greater efficiency and speed. You will no longer be distracted by the "ding" of an incoming email or the conversation of coworkers around the coffeepot. You will be able to tune out the white noise and focus on the goals at hand.

8

IMAGERY

AS HUMANS, WE ENJOY and utilize all five of our senses as we make our way through the world. And all of these sensations are imprinted in our brains in the form of memory and learning.

If you recall a certain memory, you may be able to recollect not just the pictures but the sound, the smell, the feel, and the taste. For example, you might have a good memory of a time when the family gathered at Grandma's house for Thanksgiving when you were a kid. In addition to remembering how Grandma looked in her favorite apron and the family photos on the wall, you might also remember the sound of the football game Grandpa was watching in the living room, turned up extra loud because his hearing was not so good anymore. You might remember the smell of the turkey roasting in the oven, the taste of Grandma's stuffing, and you might almost feel the scratchy wool of Grandma's woven chairs against your arms.

For many of us, our early memories shape our development, values, beliefs, and passions. They are a strong part of who we are. One of my earliest memories is of my family escaping Hungary at the end of World War II. The city of Budapest was under attack by the Soviet Union, and my father knew the best way to keep his family safe was to get out. Even now, my memories sometimes drift back to that night on the train, the bombs falling, railcars on fire, and the rush to find a safe hiding place. We were on our way to Germany, which the Americans had under control, and we could find a fresh start and try to make our way to America. That night changed my life dramatically, and the memories evoke a passion in me that has helped me keep focused in my life, like my father, working toward a goal.

Imagery is not just about making memories full of meaning. It is the mental representation of our five-sensory reality. If the images in our brains are "real" enough, they can produce the same feelings or actions as the actual object or activity you imagine. You may be more familiar with the term *visualization,* as it is often used interchangeably with imagery, but that term limits the concept to being able to "see" something in your mind. *Imagery* includes all the senses, as though you are experiencing something as it is happening.

Imagery is the number one mental skill used by elite athletes to perform at top levels. In covering the 2014 Olympic Winter Games in Sochi, Russia, the *New York Times* highlighted the use of imagery utilized by athletes. Canadian bobsledder Lyndon Rush said that before competing, he had mentally driven the Sochi course hundreds of times from start to finish. "I'll be in the shower or brushing my teeth. It just takes a minute, so I do the whole thing or sometimes just the corners that are more technical. You try to keep it fresh in your head, so when you do get there, you are not just starting at square one. It's amazing how much you can do in your mind."[1] Athletes competing in the bobsled, luge, or downhill skiing often do not get the chance to practice on the actual course until they arrive for the Games. Using imagery, like Rush, is an integral part of their training.

Practicing and improving imagery skills also helped out one of our clients, NFL kicker Billy Cundiff. "Imagery is really big for me. It's part of my prekick routine—I use it on the sidelines, and days before a game. I'm going over situations in my head of what I might face on the field, to the point where I've actually had times in a game where I thought, 'Wow, this is the exact kick I went over in my head the night before.' So I went over and replayed the kick and it was probably one of the most effortless kicks I've had in my career."[2]

Athletes are not the only peak performers who use imagery to improve their skills. Another example is the Blue Angels. This elite group of navy and marine fighter pilots awe spectators everywhere they go with their precise aerial maneuvers in F/A-18 Hornets and C-130 Hercules, often flying within mere inches of each other. For the Blue Angels, practice time in the air is limited because it is expensive and time-consuming. To supplement their practices, they use imagery. The documentary *Blue Angels: A Year in the Life* shows the group sitting around a conference room table, closing their eyes, and using imagery to go through their flight plan. The lead pilot speaks as though he were up in the air, and the rest of the team responds. They move their hands as though they are flying the plane. They are practicing as a team, working through all the steps even without being in the air. "I don't think you could do this without doing that every single day," said Commander Russ Bartlett. "There are differences in weather, winds, visibility, your mood—all those things are challenges that you try to manage so that you can fly the same exact profiles, day in and day out, at a different show site every weekend. That's hard."[3]

The skill of imagery can and should be used by everyone. It can not only improve your performance but also give you a valuable tool for coping with life's stressful situations.

THE SCIENCE OF IMAGERY

Imagery is the process of living or reliving in our minds an event, activity, or performance. The fascinating thing about imagery, which we have seen in our own trainings, and which has been documented in numerous other places, is that if the images are "real" enough, they can produce the same feelings or actions as the actual object or activity being imagined.

RIGHT BRAIN/LEFT BRAIN

The left hemisphere of our brain is utilized for logical or rational thinking, speech and verbal activity, sequential ordering, analytics, and writing. We are taught from an early age to be super analytical, and are left with little time for creative thinking. We must solve the problems, memorize lists, learn formulas, and be rational in conveying ideas. We are conditioned to think with the left brain.

The right hemisphere of our brain is used for creative thinking, imagery, intuition, emotions, and spatial relationships. By using imagery and immersing yourself in an experience, letting your body and mind go to that place, you are stimulating the right side of your brain. It is often said that we do not use our whole brains in our lives, and this is a case in point. We need to build up the right brain and develop it to successfully use imagery to become peak performers, just as we would exercise both sides of our body. This opens us up to many new possibilities for creativity and success.

REAL VS. IMAGINED

The brain and the nervous system have a difficult time differentiating between real and vivid imagined events. Therefore, we respond to imagined events in the same ways we respond to actual events. The various bodily systems respond as though the image is real, and the brain processes and remembers the image (at a neurological level) as if it is real. More specifically, vivid images actually prompt physiological, biochemical, and neurological changes in the brain and body that mirror those that happen when a person is actually experiencing an event.

To help explain this similarity, I like to use the example

of a nightmare. While we are dreaming, the images we see seem real. Think back to the last time you woke up in a cold sweat from a nightmare. What was going on inside as you startled yourself awake? Was your heart racing, your breathing rate increased, your blood pressure spiking, your muscles tense and trembling, your body sweating? Possibly you were even screaming or yelling. These are all the same physical responses we would have if the image we had experienced were real and not a dream.

A common nightmare shared by many is of toppling backward, or tripping, with the ground rushing up at us. This image is so convincing that our brains and nervous systems respond by making our arms shoot outward, hoping to slow our descent while we brace our necks, shoulders, and legs for impact—all from an image.

While you cannot see yourself sleeping, if you have a pet, you have probably been amused to see its tail wagging or its limbs twitching as though it were running, or you may even have heard muted barks and whimpers. This is similar to what we experience in the dreams where we are falling, and we jump in bed from the sensation.

IMAGERY LEADS TO PERFORMANCE

Imagery is what ties together all the modules in the peak performance program. Some individuals, during waking moments, let the physiological, biochemical, and neurological changes from imaging occur haphazardly, or in times of stress, so that images of disaster and failure invade their subconscious on a regular basis. They imagine their voices quaking when they make a speech, or somebody yawning from boredom. They imagine that they miss a tee shot or putt in golf. People can get caught up in using the wrong kind of imagery, which can undermine performance. It is important instead to leverage this mind–body relationship by visualizing yourself achieving goals and being successful.

Linking imagery to performance can bring about positive effects, including greater confidence, better attention and focus, and better stress management.

Here are some of the effects.

► Confidence

Seeing and feeling yourself successfully perform enhances confidence and motivation. Let's say you have a big presentation at work. Using imagery, you can prepare yourself mentally, ahead of time, to really ace that presentation. Let yourself imagine the room you are presenting in, and know who the people sitting in front of you are. Think about where you will sit or stand. Closing your eyes and imagining those scenes a few times before you go into that room to make the presentation will help calm you on the actual day.

Going over these images in your mind is what we call creating imagery scripts. It is not just actors who need scripts, but anyone who is facing an important performance goal.

To make a script, first decide on the end goal that you are working toward. Is it running a marathon, presenting your dissertation, or interviewing for a job? Once you identify a situation where you need to be extra focused, figure out highlights of that event. For instance, if your goal is to run a marathon, you cannot visualize the entire 26.2-mile course. But you can home in on the important parts of the course. Picture that you are off to a good start and the crowds are cheering on the side of the street; imagine the places where you will need water and get a refreshing break. Maybe you know that by mile fifteen, the run starts to take its toll on your mental health and you begin to doubt your resolve to finish. If that is the case, imagine seeing the mile fifteen marker for two minutes a day, and write an imagery script that keeps you focused on the goal of finishing and away from negative thoughts. Then highlight the end of the race. Once you underscore those important parts of what you are working toward, try imaging once a day.

▶ **Attention and Refocus**

Imagery helps you pay attention, maintain focus, and concentrate on your goal. If you have trouble focusing or find yourself getting off track, imagine yourself doing that task to completion and without distraction, and it will help you recover from that distraction more quickly. For instance, if you are giving a presentation where there were not supposed to be any questions from the audience, but somebody shot up his hand anyway and asked a really dumb question, it might throw you off and disturb your rhythm. Be prepared for the interruption through visualization. You imagine some hiccup or two to your presentation, and then create a contingency plan to prepare yourself further. For example, "When Charlie asks an off-topic question, I answer calmly and concisely and then get back to my talk."

Simulating yourself in upcoming performances and executing different strategies in your mind ahead of time are important parts of staying focused. That way when you perform the task, your brain recognizes the familiar. Rather than being in a state of vigilance for the unknown, you are comfortable in your surroundings.

▶ Stress and Energy Management

There are many amazing relaxation apps that use imagery to help you visualize every part of your body relaxing and releasing stress from your body. These techniques are often used either to clear your mind to allow sleep to come or to fill your body with energy. You can imagine where you want to be in the energy spectrum at any given time, and this can give you mental muscle memory for how you want to feel at a certain moment.

At our training center, we teach people how to breathe more slowly and lower their heart rates before they are put into a stressful energy situation; this helps give the mind energy. If you can image yourself feeling tension-free, it will promote relaxation and improve performance in any number of demanding tasks, whether it is taking your teenager out for driving lessons, interviewing for a new job, or making a big presentation.

Relaxation also boosts immune function and aids in healing and recovery. For cancer patients, imagery is an important tool. By visualizing the chemotherapy they are taking going to every part of the body and doing its job, it helps put the body in a state that is more receptive to the treatment.

PUTTING IMAGERY INTO PRACTICE

Now that we know how imagery works and the benefits it provides, here are some of the practical ways it can be used to improve your performance in all aspects of your life.

PRACTICE SKILLS

Imagery is the chance to practice more without using expensive equipment or taking up time on or in the track, field, or pool. Like the skiers and bobsledders in the Winter Olympics, many athletes are not able to practice every time on the course they will compete on or with the equipment they will use in competition. Imagery allows for the chance to build in more practice time. Imagery can also help limit bodily damage. For instance, if you are an NFL kicker, you cannot kick one thousand field goals in practice because your leg will fall off, figuratively speaking, but you can kick fifty or so, and then imagine kicking another one hundred more. Your muscles and brain will react in a similar way. Through imagery, you are gaining skills.

HEALING AND RECOVERING

Someone I know went in for spinal fusion back surgery a few years ago and was fascinated to see that his insurance company provided him with a relaxation and imagery CD a few weeks before his surgery. This insurance company had apparently seen the studies that show if you go into a surgery where you have imaged everything going great and that your doctors are highly skilled, physiologically when you are in surgery you release less stress hormones, which allows it to go better. In recovery, reactionary swelling goes down as a result, and you can imagine sending healing hormones to the area that has just been operated on.

Wounds heal nine times faster when patients are relaxed and not showing symptoms of stress. When surgery patients were given a guided imagery CD two weeks before surgery, it reduced rehabilitation and recovery costs by two thousand dollars.[4]

GENERATING BREAKTHROUGH IDEAS

Jonas Salk could not see with his own eyes how polio performed its destructive work in the body. So he imagined what it looked like in a journey as a white blood cell, moving through the body. Imagery was a part of how he was able to come up with a vaccine that would work against the disease.

At IBM, computers used to take up an entire room. Through visualizing circuit boards, engineers were able to shrink computers down to the personal computers that sit on our desks today.

Putting yourself in a new situation that might not exist yet is a process of imagery. And it is through this imagery that ideas are created and society moves forward.

CREATING A VISION

Whether you are a corporate executive or a head coach, leaders have a concrete message to get across to their teams and the general public about their missions. However, most people do not sit down and read lengthy mission statements day in and day out. That is where visualizing and imagery can help. For example, take the Apple logo from a few years ago, which was a rainbow-colored apple and the two words "Think Different." It was successful because it conveyed to people the meaning of thinking outside the box, about what is new, and what can be changed. This way of thinking applies to everyone who works for Apple and everyone who buys their products.

Another example is FedEx's slogan: Moving Forward. For consumers and employees, that is not only what they do—move things—but also how they think. The arrow in the logo exemplifies this. A core visual of a mission can help employees understand and work toward a specific goal, day in and day out.

SEE YOUR SUCCESS

When working with clients to improve their imagery skills, we first begin with writing a short imagery script about their outcome goal. Let's say that goal is to lose ten pounds. The tools to get to that goal include working out five days a week, eating healthfully, and shopping for healthy foods. We help the person imagine vivid scenes for each of these tools using all five senses, with reminders that will help him stay on track. For instance, we work into the script a commute to work where he drives past a donut shop that he wants to avoid, or a reminder to keep a gym bag in the car, or seeing himself working out during commercials instead of snacking when he watches TV.

Writing a script and creating images is incredibly important to becoming a peak performer. If you cannot imagine things like being able to fit into your old jeans, graduating from college, or speaking in public, then there is no neuron connection in your brain for that scenario to exist. With no pathway, that scenario becomes impossible to fulfill. Even if you do not believe it yet, practice something that is not possible. Make neuron connections happen. This is a really powerful tool.

When bestselling motivational author Wayne Dyer first conceived of his next book project, he would think of the finished cover first. He had the book cover designed and wrapped the book jacket around an old book. Then, with a visual incarnation of his new book in front of him, he wrote the content to go inside. If you can see it, you can make it happen.

PUTTING IT INTO PRACTICE

You go to the gym to lift weights and do cardio, all while eating the right foods, just to stay healthy. But what are you doing to work out your brain?

"The physical aspect of the game can only take you so far," said Olympic gold-medal-winning gymnast Shannon Miller. "The mental aspect has to kick in, especially when you're talking about the best of the best. In the Olympic Games, everyone is talented. Everyone trains hard. Everyone does the work. What separates the gold medalists from the silver medalists is simply the mental game."[5]

Two important steps in setting outcome goals are as follows:

1. Have a clear vision and mission, and be able to articulate both.
2. Be able to translate that mission into outcome, performance, and process goals.

The process takes you from your "dream" to clear actions that have to be taken in order to reach your goals. It involves developing the necessary commitment, evaluating potential barriers to goal attainment, and working through them, constructing action plans that take you step-by-step toward your goal.

Here are some ways to improve your mental game and help you become a peak performer. The following exercises help work the right side of your brain, improving its function and enabling your imagery skills to grow.

EXERCISE ONE

Take a minute and imagine that you are walking through your childhood bedroom. See the colors and patterns of your bedroom. What do you hear in the house, or through the window? Remember what it is like to lie down on the bed and how that feels—is the bed soft or lumpy or hard? What is your view from the bed? Where are your clothes kept? Are any favorite toys lying around? What does your room smell like?

EXERCISE TWO

Picture you are holding on to an empty bucket in one arm. Then imagine shoveling sand into it until it is half-full. How does that feel? Is your arm tired as you are still holding this bucket? Now shovel more sand into the bucket, so it is really heavy now. What does it feel like? Are your fingers straining to hold the handle? Does your shoulder ache? Is your body tilting over to accommodate the weight? Are your lips and tongue dry from the exertion? Do you feel hot? Can you smell the sand in the metal bucket?

EXERCISE THREE

Imagine that you have an orange in your hands. How does it feel? How does it smell? Now cut into it, and see what it looks like inside; feel the juice running onto your hands. Then imagine you bite into it. What does it taste like? Are your lips puckering, or are you salivating?

IMAGERY PRACTICE: THE BEACH

You are walking on the beach and can hear the waves crashing onto the shore. You feel the sand on your feet, and can taste the salt spray on your tongue. The wind is blowing your hair, and you lie down on a soft towel. The sand molds around your body. The sun gently warms you, and you pull a hat down over your face to give you shade.

IMAGERY PRACTICE: THE BOOKSHELF

Look at your bookshelf for ten seconds, and then close your eyes. See if you can place in your head where each book was in order. This helps with visual memory.

IMAGERY PRACTICE: THE WALK-THROUGH

Walk through a room, taking in as many things as you can with a timer. With your phone, set an alarm for the number of seconds that it took you to walk through that room, and try to complete it in the same time span.

EXTERNAL IMAGERY PRACTICE

The imagery practices we have been doing have been from the point of view of the person who is doing them. Now try to picture how you look from an outsider's perspective. For instance, a dancer may think her work looks great from her position on the stage, but from the audience's, she might be turned in a way so that they cannot appreciate the full beauty of the dance. Seeing yourself from the outside allows your brain to view what is supposed to be happening within you, and it will build up the connections for a beautiful performance.

9

PRACTICE METHODS

THROUGHOUT MY LIFE, DEFINING moments and opportunities arose where my own preparation helped me successfully manage each situation and be ready to take advantage of the opportunities. My years at West Point and training from other leaders in the army helped me be prepared to make the quick decisions necessary on the battlefield to protect my company and lead us in successful missions against the enemy. Taking advantage of educational opportunities helped me be prepared for career advances that led me to the place where I could pursue my own research.

Practicing the skills in the Five-Point Plan will help you be prepared for the defining moments and opportunities that arise in your life. When those moments come, I want you to be able to have your thought processes fine-tuned and ready to make your best decisions when it matters most. It is important to follow the steps of our training process.

At Apex Performance, we have high-tech ways of teaching these methods. We connect our clients to sensors that measure responses to stress, and help our clients analyze those results and work on the practices needed to improve them. But readers who do not have access to our training centers, and those who have completed the training but have graduated from our centers, need to be able to practice at home. Ultimately, these tools are to guide you to be able to put into practice the skills you learn at any time and in any situation.

Let's start with the first step to putting all this into practice. To begin, I suggest you record a scripted relaxation tape, using our suggestions in Chapter 6. We know from research that stress can cloud our judgment, but people are able to make better decisions when in a relaxed state in which they can calmly review all the scenarios and options. By practicing relaxation methods, you will be able to remain calm in intense situations.

Once you have your relaxation script, the next step is to practice triggering your relaxation response with a combination of techniques including audio, breathing, body position, a positive mindset, and imagery.

Using your brain to control your body's response to situations is a powerful tool. The brain and the heart are very much linked, and learning to lower your heart rate and control your own physiology can transform stress and anxiety into creativity and positive energy.

Learning to relax is a step-by-step process:

1. Find a quiet environment with little to no distractions.

2. Get into a comfortable position, preferably lying down or sitting in a comfortable chair.

3. Practice deep, rhythmic breathing. Inhale through your nose slowly, for four to five seconds; then exhale through your mouth slowly, another four to five seconds. The longer you exhale, the more it slows the heart rate.

4. Find a passive mind—allow distracting thoughts to come and go. Empty your mind of distractions so you are not thinking about anything.

5. Go to your "happy place." Enjoy your imagery, whether it is of the beach, a quiet place in the mountains, or anywhere that you find relaxing.

After you have gone through these steps, measure your breathing. You're looking for a rate of six to eight breaths per minute, as compared with a normal twelve to twenty breaths per minute. Set a stopwatch when you feel that you are in a slow and deeper rate of breathing, and, without disturbing your mindset, count the number of breaths you take.

Keep practicing, so you know what this calm feels like. If you find yourself still not able to reach this slower, deeper pace, try watching a clock or counting out each inhale (four to five seconds) and exhale (four to five seconds) for two to three minutes, so you can get a sense of how it should feel. Because you are most likely dramatically slowing down your usual breathing rate, this may feel uncomfortable at first, and even labored until you get adjusted. Hang in there—with regular, daily practice, your body will begin to adapt to this ideal pattern and you will not have to try so hard to make it happen. Practicing to the point where you can feel yourself getting to a calm state is crucial, because once you have mastered this you will be able to apply this technique to get yourself into a relaxed state prior to a performance situation.

Another way of measuring your biomechanics is with instruments that use advanced biofeedback technology. There are a number of easy-to-use sensors on the market that allow you to track your heart rate and rhythm and produce results that you can use to monitor your progress with reaching synchronization between your mental, emotional, and physical states.

Another concrete way of measuring your performance is by using brain-training programs. Some good ones are available online, including Lumosity, Fit Brains, and BrainHQ. These programs provide training through different games and activities. You can create programs designed specifically for your own mental requirements and skill set. You can improve and track your mental skills, such as flexibility in thinking, brain speed, and accuracy. Sign up for a trial, and keep track of your baseline score.

If you practice brain training online with these games and activities, combine it with the Five-Point Plan, and practice getting yourself into a relaxed performance state before you start the game; you should show improvement in just ten days. We are only talking about twenty to thirty minutes each day of brain training plus practicing your breathing (remember: short, three- to five-minute sessions several times throughout the day to get that high-quality, repetitive practice). These small endeavors can make a huge impact! Play around with different times in your schedule to challenge yourself, especially when you are not at your best so you can see what it takes to get you into that ideal, focused performance state. The industry standard for these programs is a 20 percent improvement in thirty days. If you follow our program studiously, you can compare yourself with others and see your gains compared with other participants. There is something to be said for competition!

I use all our models in my everyday life. Learning the skills needed for peak performance is not good for just business but for your personal life as well. For instance, I am a nervous flyer, but I must fly all the time. I use imagery and stress management exercises together with coherence biofeedback at the airport during preboarding and prior to takeoff to help overcome those feelings of anxiety and stress.

Through research and personal practice, I have come up with some other techniques that help improve mental stamina.

One simple way to retrain your brain is through finger tapping. Tap your fingers of each hand in the opposite direction at the same time. In other words, start with the thumb of your right hand and the pinky finger of your left hand and tap from left to right with each hand at the same time. Going through this exercise, doing the opposite of what feels natural, helps to "retrain the brain" and sharpens your focus.

Another good way of using your attention control is to listen to classical music. I am a big fan of Mozart, but you might enjoy Bach or Beethoven. It does not matter who; just choose who you enjoy. While listening, pick out one instrument and follow it through the whole piece. Then listen to it again, picking out a different instrument to follow. There is a world of difference from what the clarinets are doing to what the flutes are playing, not to mention the violins.

During times of stress, I use imagery to put myself on a beautiful beach—my favorite place in the world. I use all my senses to feel my toes in the sand and the ocean breeze on my face, taste the salt from the sea air, feel the heat from the sun on my skin, hear the waves crashing and seagulls singing, and smell the suntan lotion and air around me. Going to this happy place helps me relax, enabling me to be in the right frame of mind to tackle anything that might come my way.

The human brain is an amazing tool full of possibilities. Many of us are not working at our full potential because we have not learned how to control our brains. We go through the motions of our daily lives without thinking about how small steps could make big improvements. That is why I feel it is so important to share our five-step program for peak performance. By learning about goal setting, adaptive thinking, stress and energy management, attention control, and imagery, and practicing these techniques in your daily life, you can activate parts of your brain you were not consciously using before. You will open up new doors and find new opportunities, both in your career and in your personal life. By teaching yourself to live in the moment, focus on what you are doing, and reduce your overall stress, you will find yourself happier, able to make better decisions, and working at your full potential. You will be able to perform at your best in performance situations, face leadership challenges, and excel at making decisions. With these techniques, anyone can be a peak performer.

10

PEAK
PERFORMANCE
APPLIED

NOW THAT YOU HAVE LEARNED the tools of peak performers, and the practices to help incorporate them into your own mental strategies, it is time to apply them in real-world scenarios. The real world is not a pretty one nowadays. It is a world characterized by four major barrier forces: *V*olatility, *U*ncertainty, *C*omplexity, and *A*mbiguity. First highlighted by the U.S. Army War College and the National Defense University in alerting the armed forces to the nature of war fighting in the future, these are key characteristics of today's performance environment. The acronym VUCA became a popular way of depicting the nature and impact of these forces, and was integrated into the lexicon of strategic thinking and planning.[1] Let's look at it more closely.

. . .

VOLATILITY

Volatility is characterized by explosive change. Volatility calls for vision. Leaders need to visualize and "see" potentialities and possibilities. Volatility impacts an organization by creating fear and an aversion to taking needed risks. Volatility leads to reverting back to basics. Peter Vaill, professor of management at Antioch University, known for his innovative approaches to organizational behavior, coined the phrase *permanent white water* in his book *Learning as a Way of Being* to describe the rate of environmental change in the world as we know it.[2]

UNCERTAINTY

Uncertainty is about the unpredictability of change. Will things stay the same for two weeks, or change tomorrow? Executives in the food distribution industry, highly dependent on gas as a means of business, are well versed in the uncertainty of our times. Should we raise prices of our product to make up for high gas prices? Or should we not risk alienating customers when the cost of gas might go down? It is also about when people have a lack of clarity and awareness of what is happening, and cannot get a grasp on understanding the issues and events. Uncertainty calls for understanding. Leaders need to be comfortable being uncomfortable. Uncertainty can cause paralysis by analysis— not doing anything in a ceaseless quest to understand first.

COMPLEXITY

Complexity is about the intricacies of key decision factors, the multiplicity of forces and events, and the chaos that can surround an organization. Public relations companies are faced with complexity in today's world. Gone are the days when a great media campaign meant coming up with good radio and television spots. Today's marketers need to be well versed in Internet advertising and social media. And the job of marketing is ongoing; it does not stop once the campaign is launched. Real people need to handle tweets and Facebook posts in real time, reacting to current events in a way that is appropriate for the company. Complexity causes a search for black-and-white solutions when none might exist. Our instinct is to revert back to the time before the chaos, when things were simpler. But success comes from moving forward. Complexity calls for clarity and an ability to see solutions.

AMBIGUITY

Ambiguity means that there will be a sense of vagueness about the current situation and potential outcomes. There will be a lack of certainty about the meaning of an event. For instance, was the Ebola outbreak in West Africa going to be a pandemic, or could it be contained? Ambiguity exists when a given event or situation can be interpreted in more than one way. It is the confusion over reality and its potential for misreading events, especially over cause and effect. Leaders need to develop flexibility, agility, and decisiveness to exercise intuitive decision making. Ambiguity calls for action.

PEAK LEADERSHIP

Achieving sustained high performance in such a world is a daunting task. Traditional emphases on organizational and workplace solutions for meeting challenges have not produced the desired results in performance improvement and productivity increases. These methods have typically focused on peripheral issues and have not addressed the heart of the challenge, which is how to fundamentally change the manner in which people approach their own performances and tap into their full potential.

Leadership performance excellence can be viewed from three different levels.

Organizational leadership would be the CEO of a company or the division commander of an army division. At this level, the leadership is more indirect and calls for some leadership competencies that are different from the other two levels. Vision and clarity of strategic thinking become paramount. The capability to see the big picture and not get bogged down with details is essential. This level of leadership influences organizational performance.

The next level is *leading others*. This involves leading small teams, small units, special projects, and so forth. This level of direct leadership is defined by both unit size and the extent of direct contact between the leader and followers on a regular daily basis. This level of leadership directly influences team performance. It is at this level that the leader has the most direct personal influence.

Self-leadership is the ability to control and manage oneself, and it affects individual performance within the organization. This is where concepts like self-discipline, self-control, and self-mastery come into play. A key principle taught at West Point is that you cannot successfully lead others until you are able to "lead yourself," so our focus will be on this.

SELF-LEADERSHIP IS ABOUT INNER CONTROL

The ability to be in "the zone," to focus on the present with no thought of the past or future, concentrating only on what you are doing, not on how you are doing, is fundamental to all levels of leadership. By practicing the skills learned earlier, you will be able to focus better, throughout all the turmoil and upheavals and pressure that is omnipresent in today's work environment.

The Five-Point Plan is your tool to inner control. Setting goals focuses your direction and gives you a clear point to work toward. Then, through practicing and improving your mental agility when it comes to positive effect thinking, stress and energy management, attention control, and imagery, you improve your overall mental abilities. When you are calm and confident in your own mind, it is only natural that you exude those characteristics to others, which are important qualities of any good leader.

In real-world, day-to-day scenarios, you may be called on to utilize any one of the five different techniques, or you might find yourself using multiple techniques in conjunction with one another. Increasing your mental capabilities provides you with the strength you need to meet the challenges of your daily environment.

REAL VUCA WORLD PEAK PERFORMANCES

Given the inherent challenges of a business world filled with complexity and volatility, CEOs have identified *creativity* as the number one leadership quality that is essential for traversing this kind of environment. Creative leaders can bring qualities that are uniquely made for this kind of a business challenge. According to a study by IBM, creative leaders seek "disruptive innovation, consider unorthodox ways to change the enterprise, are comfortable with ambiguity, and are courageous and visionary enough to make dramatic decisions that change the status quo."[3]

What is essential for leaders to thrive in a VUCA performance environment? Good leaders must respond quickly and effectively to challenges from rapidly evolving, ever-changing situations. They must do this by providing vision, direction, simplicity, a sense of control, and confidence. For this kind of turbulent performance environment, leaders need to possess the following capacities:

- Situational awareness
- Mental agility
- Learned instinct
- Commander's calm

The challenge for leaders is to be especially effective in extreme conditions. Anything less will not carry the day. Leaders owe it to the organizations they serve and the people they lead to bring their very best to the challenges faced in high-pressure and high-demand situations. Anyone who has ever served as a leader in a VUCA environment quickly comes to realize that much of what they knew and learned was insufficient. I have been in such situations and quickly realized that I needed more to get me through. I had to reach within myself for something deeper, something that reflected who I was, not just what I knew and what I did. In a VUCA environment, leaders need to be at their best as the person they are, harnessing the power of who they have become over the years. Personal strengths such as confidence, adaptability, agility, calm, and focus will carry the day far more than competencies or skills, knowledge and abilities, or desired behavior lists.

DEVELOPING PERFORMANCE CAPACITIES
WITH MENTAL SKILLS

How do the mental skills you have learned interact to best develop the performance capacities of situational awareness, mental agility, learned instinct, and commander's calm? They all have a part in the overall development of each of the capacities, with some playing a greater role than others.

Situational awareness requires exceptional attention control, learning to "pay attention to *how* you pay attention" and razor-sharp focus. Imagery provides an intuitive sense for what is happening around us. It is much quicker than the normal thought processes we use for analyzing and solving problems and thus a powerful tool for developing situational awareness.

Mental agility incorporates elements of adaptive thinking, attention control, and imagery. Flexible and fluid thinking are critical in a constantly changing situation. Staying focused on what is most important regardless of the distractions enhances the ability to shift quickly and seamlessly between tasks. Using the power of imagery to envision possible outcomes before they happen provides the plasticity for rapid assessment and decision making.

Learned instinct is what drives intuitive and gut-feeling types of decisions and execution. We actually operate with "three brains": the brain in the head, the brain in the heart, and the brain in the gut. Recent research has demonstrated that the heart and the gut have nervous systems and thus are able to "think." We can become more intuitive and instinctive in our actions by listening and trusting what the heart and gut have to "say." Such instinctive behavior can be learned and developed through repetitive, deliberate practice and experiences that directly target elements of the heart and gut that affect what we do and how we do it.

Finally, we are all familiar with the cool, calm, and collected commander who never seems ruffled by anything. *Commander's calm* can best be developed by learning to directly control the mental, emotional, and physiological responses to stressful and high arousal situations. It is keeping the fight-or-flight response in check. It is not so much about trying to control events as it is about controlling yourself, especially your thoughts, self-talk, and emotions. Learning self-regulation to minimize stress responses and optimize energy levels that match the situation is crucial to remaining calm in high-stress situations. With today's much more sophisticated yet accessible biofeedback and neurofeedback technologies, the ability to control otherwise involuntary mechanisms is a potent tool for performing at our best when it matters the most, and it matters the most under extreme conditions.

Following are real-world situations demonstrating each of the skill sets.

SITUATIONAL AWARENESS
||||||||||||||||||||||||||||||||||||||||||||||||||||||||||||||||||||||||||||||||||||||||||||

Definition: perceiving salient elements of a rapidly changing environment in order to anticipate, understand, and act on future events

Application of the Five-Point Plan: The combination of improved positive-effective thinking and attention control improve a person's ability to have situational awareness and make good choices when decisions need to be made.

NORTHWEST FLIGHT 188

At 5:41 p.m., October 21, 2009, Northwest Flight 188 departed from San Diego bound for Minneapolis. As the Airbus 320 flew to an altitude of thirty-seven thousand feet, the crew made regular contact with Denver air traffic controllers. A short time later when Denver air traffic control tried to reestablish contact with them, there was no response from the cockpit. Controllers tried texting the crew: nothing. At 7:56 p.m., the FAA designated the flight NORDO status, short for no radio communications. Denver center handed off tracking responsibilities to Minneapolis center. Controllers in Minneapolis could not make radio contact either. Fighter jets were mobilized in Madison, Wisconsin, with fears mounting that Flight 188 might have been hijacked.

Four and a half hours after takeoff, this plane was

supposed to descend, but it never did. It kept on flying. It flew over Minneapolis and kept right on going. Flight 188 overshot Minneapolis by more than 150 miles. There had been no radio contact for more than an hour. Finally at 9:14 p.m., air traffic controllers were able to connect with the crew. By that time the plane was well past Minneapolis and over Wisconsin. Controllers asked the pilot to make a 180-degree turn and ordered him to make a series of maneuvers to make sure he was in control of the aircraft, not hijackers.

The pilot's explanation for overshooting Minneapolis? The National Transportation Safety Board said, "The crew stated they were in a heated discussion over airline policy and they lost situational awareness."[4] At 10:02 p.m., the plane finally landed safely in Minneapolis, one hour and fourteen minutes late. This was a frightening demonstration of the loss of situational awareness.

I want to make a specific point about the difficulty of having situational awareness in especially routine and often dull attention tasks. In such situations, it is difficult to maintain a high level of alertness and stay narrowly focused. For example, in fairness to the pilots on Flight 188, once the takeoff is complete, the plane flies itself for the most part, and the pilot has little to do other than remain aware. In such a circumstance, it would be easy to get distracted by some other interest, as was the case here.

Another example would be security guards watching an array of security monitors. Imagine spending endless hours watching these monitors and nothing happens. Boredom quickly sets in, and attention wanders. Some companies have become creative by inserting some sort of action or visual change into some of the monitors. This periodic change on the monitors keeps the security guards more aware and alert, and reduces the possibility of boredom and reduced vigilance.

Being aware of our surroundings, having the ability to recognize a constantly changing situation, and remaining focused on what is important are critical attention survival mechanisms that begin at birth and continue to develop with experience. Without them, we would be unable to respond with the appropriate thoughts, feelings, and actions. As we develop, we become increasingly more proficient at attending to the right thing at the right time. However, at some point, we discover that the normal development of our attention is no longer sufficient to meet new and ever-changing challenges as the world becomes more and more complex and the demand for our attention increases exponentially.

Highly successful performers discover ways they can accelerate the development of their ability to focus and concentrate. This is crucial, especially for situations that are unclear and ambiguous, where recognizing and understanding the most relevant information and then being able to act on it are paramount. Everything begins with attention or inattention. The practices outlined in Chapter

9 can help you improve your own abilities to maintain attention. For example, it matters little how adept you are at making decisions or how much problem solving you know if you are attending to the wrong thing! Focus comes first, then awareness, and then action.

Lack of situational awareness has been identified as a primary factor in poor decision making and in accidents attributed to human error.[5] This is especially true for work areas where the flow of information is very high and the consequences for inattention and making poor decisions is serious. The required level of attentiveness in any given situation is determined by the performance demands of that situation and the inherent distractions that accompany it. As we grow and develop in our personal and professional lives, we take on added roles and responsibilities that require concurrent improvements in our ability to pay attention. For example, firefighters learn what to pay attention to in their unique environment, police officers and soldiers in theirs, organizational leaders in theirs, and so on. This is necessary and provides the attention framework for accomplishing the desired tasks.

However, as a situation becomes more unpredictable and unclear, more like a VUCA world, situational awareness based on past training and experience becomes much more difficult. There will come a point where ambiguity and lack of clarity leave little to go by in terms of where to look, what to listen for, what to focus on. Some of the skills, tools, and techniques offered in this book will go a long way in developing situational awareness in volatile, uncertain, complex, and ambiguous situations.

MENTAL AGILITY

Definition: the ability to apply a creative solution to a complex problem in a timely manner

Application of the Five-Point Plan: Setting goals, controlling stress, having confidence in one's decisions, and being able to maintain focus all work together in helping improve a person's mental agility.

A CRITICAL PICKUP IN AFGHANISTAN[6]

In November 2003, a U.S.-led coalition launched Operation Mountain Resolve in the Nuristan and Kunar Provinces of Afghanistan in order to disrupt anti-coalition militia operations and prevent militia members from seeking sanctuary in the rugged Afghan provinces. Members of the Tenth Mountain division called for a CH–47 helicopter to pick up Afghan Persons Under Custody (prisoners). Pilot Larry Murphy, Company G, 104th Aviation Regiment of the Pennsylvania Guard, answered the call. Upon arriving at the scene, Capt. Murphy quickly recognized the extreme ruggedness of the terrain with rocks and sharp slopes all around. Tenth Mountain soldiers had assembled the Afghan persons in custody for evacuation on a small

rooftop, precariously perched on the side of a cliff. It became quickly evident that there was no other place for the
helicopter to land.

Very much aware of the urgency of the evacuation and
the speed with which he needed to accomplish this so that
U.S. soldiers were minimally exposed to possible enemy
fire, Capt. Murphy gently hovered and then set the back
end of the helicopter down on the rooftop while keeping
the front end hovering in midair. Experts tell us that this
was close to impossible. As noted by one seasoned helicopter pilot, "Now how many people on the planet you reckon
could set the ass end of a chopper down on the rooftop of
a shack on a steep mountain cliff and hold it there while
soldiers load prisoners in the rear?"[7]

Note that the definition of *mental agility* has three parts to
it: creative solution, complex problem, and timely manner.
All three are required if one is to be mentally agile. Mental
agility is about being fluid, flexible, and adaptive in what
and how you think about a situation. It determines how
well you can come to a quick solution and decision, and
how quickly you can act on it. The chopper pilot in the
Afghanistan evacuation story clearly demonstrated the
presence of all three.

Mental agility is developing the mind to move swiftly
and correctly. It is about having a balance between speed
and accuracy as we process and work to understand an

ever-increasing barrage of information. Optimizing both in a rapidly changing and uncertain situation is essential. As mentioned earlier, a key part of mental agility is what and how you think, and a large part of that is how well you control your thoughts in the moment. The bad news is this is difficult. The good news is control can be taught and developed, as you have seen in the practices laid out in previous chapters. That control can become just as automatic as your other instinctive responses. In reality, *it is not what is happening to you that matters, but how you think about what is happening.*

Adaptive thinking builds greater capacity for displaying mental agility. It places much greater emphasis on training *how* to think, rather than just *what* to think. The meaning of the oft-used phrase *thinking out of the box* is a useful way to describe adaptive thinking. To *think out of the box* requires openness to new and different ideas and perspectives. It provides more insight into the strengths and weaknesses of one's own thinking. To be adaptive is to recognize not only the various parts of a given situation but also the possible patterns derived from various combinations of these parts. The gestalt principle, *the whole is greater than the sum of its parts,* is an important element of mental agility. Pattern recognition is a critical brain function mechanism. Some of our best thinking is achieved when we understand causes, connect those causes, and then make sense out of them. In a VUCA environment, causality is difficult, but not impossible, to discern. Since the brain likes patterns, anything we can do to help it make connections is worth our effort. Making connections can be trained. It is the brain's most natural function.

Mental agility means thinking while performing. It means developing fast and simple heuristics, simple rules of thumb that fit the environment in which they are used. In an uncertain and hard-to-predict environment, decisions still have to be made, but it will be much more difficult. In such environments, highly successful performers learn and use trial and error. The brain's pattern recognition bias aids in the ability to develop such rules of thumb.

LEARNED INSTINCT

Definition: taking action based on learned behaviors that become automatic in time through repetitive, deliberate, and repeated practice and experience

Application of the Five-Point Plan: The repeated practice of skills necessary in the Five-Point Plan turn those mental skills into learned instinct that helps you succeed in times of stress and volatility.

US AIRWAYS FLIGHT 1549, MIRACLE ON THE HUDSON[8]

On January 15, 2009, US Airways Flight 1549 left New York's LaGuardia Airport, heading for Charlotte, North Carolina, with 155 people on board. Just minutes into the flight, the airplane encountered a flock of geese. The pilot had no choice but to fly straight through the flock of geese. Still ascending, the bird strike caused both engines to fail, leaving the plane without power. Capt. Chelsey "Sully" Sullenberger, the pilot, immediately radioed back to LaGuardia Airport and described the situation and asked for instructions to return to LaGuardia. As the plane turned around and descended with both engines off, the plane flew over the Hudson River, heading back toward the airport. Capt. Sully realized he was not going to make it to LaGuardia and made an instant and instinctive decision to land the airplane in the Hudson River. With a near-perfect glider-like desent, the plane skidded across the water and came to a halt totally intact and afloat. Emergency procedures had been started by the crew at three thousand feet, actions that are normally accomplished at thirty thousand feet in an emergency. All 155 passengers exited the airplane safely and were rescued by boats in the vicinity. To gain a real appreciation for how this potential disaster unfolded, here is the actual conversation among Capt. Sully, an air traffic controller (ATC), and the airport tower (Tower).

[ATC] Cactus 15-four-niner departure to contact, maintain one-five thousand.

[Capt. Sully] Maintain one-five thousand, Cactus 15-four-niner.

[ATC] Cactus 15-four-niner turn left heading 270.

[Capt. Sully] This is Cactus 15-four-niner. Hit birds through . . . *(garbled)*, turning back towards LaGuardia.

[ATC] OK. You need to return to LaGuardia. Turn left heading 220.

[Capt. Sully] 220.

[ATC] Stop all departures. He's got an emergency returning.

[Tower] Who is it?

[ATC] It's 1549. A bird strike. He lost all engines. He lost thrust in both engines. Returning immediately.

[Tower] Cactus 1549. Which engines?

[ATC] He lost thrust in both engines, he said.

[Tower] Got it.

[ATC] Cactus 1549. Could you get here? Do you want to try to land on 1R13?

[Capt. Sully] We are unable. We may end up in the Hudson.

[ATC] Cactus 1549. There's going to be less traffic to runway 31.

[Capt. Sully] Unable. *(Pilot makes decision to try to land in the Hudson River.)*

[ATC] OK what do you need to land? Do you want to try to go to Teterboro?

[Capt. Sully] Yes.

[ATC] Teterboro, aahh . . . *(garbled)* LaGuardia emergency inbound. Cactus 1549 over the George Washington Bridge, wants to go to your airport right now.

[Teterboro Tower] Wants our airport. Check. Does he need assistance?

[ATC] Ah yes, it was a bird strike. Can I get him in on runway 1?

[Teterboro Tower] Runway 1. That's good.

[ATC] Cactus 1549, turn right 28 zero. You can land on runway 1 at Teterboro.

[Capt. Sully] We can't do it.

[ATC] OK. Which runway would you like at Teterboro?

[Capt. Sully] We're gonna be in the Hudson.

[ATC] I'm sorry. Say again Cactus. Cactus 1549, radar contact is lost. *(3:31. Plane lands in the Hudson River.)* You also got Newark airport at two o'clock in about seven miles. Eagle 2718 . . . *(garbled)* 210.

[UNKNOWN] 210. 2718. I think he said he was going in the Hudson.

[ATC] Cactus 1549. You still on? *(Silence)*

I have provided the transcript of the conversation among the tower, another air traffic controller, and Capt. Sully to highlight two key points: the disconnect between the tower and air controllers and Capt. Sully, and the calm and poise Capt. Sully demonstrated as he made his almost matter-of-fact decision to land in the Hudson. He later said in an interview, "It was very quiet as we worked, my copilot and I. We were a team. But to have zero thrust coming out of those engines was shocking—the silence."[9] Sullenberger calmly walked the nonflooded part of the passenger cabin twice to make sure everyone had evacuated before retrieving the plane's maintenance logbook and leaving the aircraft, the last to evacuate.

From where did this calm and poise come? His pilot training? Was it something inherently different about Capt. Sully? If ever there was an example of instinctive behavior in a critical situation, the actions and demeanor of Capt. Sully certainly exemplified it. To answer these questions, we need to know a little about his background. In addition to his years of experience as a US Airways pilot, his record speaks volumes of experience as an instructor and aviation accident investigator. But these are not the primary reasons for his heroic deed.

What makes this a good story about learned instinct is that Capt. Sully holds a Commercial Pilot Certificate rating in gliders! As a cadet at the U.S. Air Force Academy, Class of 1969, he was selected as one of a dozen other freshmen to start a cadet glider club. By the end of that first year, he was already a glider instructor pilot. Capt. Sully continued flying gliders throughout his career and served as a master glider pilot instructor. This experience played an immense role in his success in landing Flight 1549. Dr. Frank Ayers, chairman of the flight department at Embry-Riddle Aeronautical University in Daytona Beach, Florida, said this of Sully's glider experience: "It certainly would help, because in a glider, every landing is an engine-out landing." To safely land Flight 1549 on the frigid Hudson River, as with other water landings, Sullenberger had to fly "as slow as you can without diving," Ayers said, adding that the process is similar to landing a glider.[10]

In other words, through a long period of deliberate and repetitive practice, Capt. Sully honed his skills flying a powerless airplane. His actions became automatic and instinctive. What he was able to do on that day over the Hudson was learned instinct. It was a situation that required an instant, automatic response, not thinking.

So what is this idea of "learned instinct"? We are all familiar with the idea of basic instincts and how critical they are to our very survival. The most basic instincts are inborn and come with our genetic blueprints. They are triggered automatically. We also recognize that there are many other responses in our behavioral repertoire that are also automatic, also seemingly "instinctive." We all use phrases like "gut instinct" or "go with your instincts," or "my gut tells me." Have you ever thought about what that really means?

The fact is that we can and do develop learned instincts. In addition to the repetitive and deliberate practice, developing learned instincts also requires the controlled use of the "nervous systems" of the heart and the gut. As detailed earlier in this chapter, recent neuroscience discoveries tell us that both the heart and the gut have nervous systems, and can be trained to react in certain situations, especially when you know how to control those reactions with your mind.

Until recently, a common method for training in the U.S. Army has been through rote repetition. Rote repetition is basically running through an exercise or training activity over and over again in hopes of changing behavior and improving performance. For example, a typical training activity for a squad of soldiers would be the clearing of a room in a hostile building. This can be practiced on nearly every army base in simulated buildings and rooms. In this training exercise, the squad would enter the room in a specified formation with each member carrying out assigned roles. During a typical exercise, a sergeant would run the soldiers through the simulation over and over and over again until they get it right.

This kind of training is much akin to Einstein's definition of insanity, "doing the same thing over and over again while hoping for a different outcome." Today, that exercise looks very different. Instead of just repeating the exercise over and over, the sergeant will give deliberate and targeted instructions each time the soldiers clear the room. Targeted means having a clear and specified goal for each and every repetition. The brain learns through repetition, but not just any kind of repetition. It learns best through repetitive deliberate practice, which means that each and every repetition must have a specific and defined goal.

We know from neuroscience that the brain's prefrontal cortex, the part of the brain that is responsible for executive function—judgment, problem-solving ability, and so on—works most efficiently and effectively when it has a clear and precise goal or target. Learned instinctive behavior is developed primarily through repetition. We now know it is not any kind of repetition but deliberate practice that incorporates a specific and precise goal with every repetition.

In building the leader capacity of learned instinct, we develop core mental skills that contribute significantly in developing automatic learned behaviors. For example, with setting goals we learn the importance of having clear and precise targets for our behavior. Having a clear goal helps shape the precise behaviors needed to achieve that goal. Since automaticity develops best with simplicity and precision, a good goal-setting process can contribute to that. Voluntary control and regulation of involuntary autonomic nervous system mechanisms (fight-or-flight response) are critical for developing learned "instinctive" behaviors. Recognizing attention cues and being able to direct our attention to them is key in any situation, but especially in critical situations.

COMMANDER'S CALM

Definition: responding mentally, emotionally, and physiologically in a cool, calm, and collected manner

Application of the Five-Point Plan: Positive-effective thinking, stress and energy management, attention control, and imagery all play important roles in a person exhibiting commander's calm.

GENERAL DWIGHT D. EISENHOWER AND D-DAY AT NORMANDY[11]

D-day was the first day of any military operation during the war. Over the years, however, the expression *D-day* has come to mean the greatest single Allied operation of World War II, the invasion of Normandy. In the spring of 1944, Allied forces engaged in a massive buildup on the British Isles. They were preparing to launch Operation Overlord, the invasion of France. General Dwight D. Eisenhower, the Allied Supreme Commander in Europe, had to make one of the most critical decisions of World War II, the date for the invasion, and time was quickly running out. Hundreds of thousands of Allied troops, sailors, and airmen awaited his orders to begin Operation Overlord. Eisenhower had already delayed Overlord for a month. He postponed other military operations to allow the Allies time to build their forces and amass the landing craft they needed. A date was set: June 5, 1944. General Eisenhower gave orders for all officers and men to be ready. However, there was one factor that was very troubling and it was beyond the Allies' control. The weather.

The Allied planners knew they could not control the

weather for D-day. Late on the evening of June 2, 1944, Eisenhower, his top generals, and British Prime Minister Winston Churchill met to review the weather forecast. The news was not good—D-day, June 5, promised cloudy skies, rain, and heavy seas. Under such conditions, the invasion stood little chance of success. Under tremendous pressure from both those who wanted to go and those who said wait for a better weather period (later in June), Eisenhower decided to wait another day to see if weather conditions might improve. Less than twenty-four hours before the scheduled invasion, Eisenhower gathered his advisers again. The forecast indicated that the rain would stop and there would be breaks in the clouds by midafternoon on June 5.

With the massive buildup weighing heavily on his mind, Eisenhower calmly and decidedly changed the date for D-day to June 6. He knew that the tides would not favor an invasion again for nearly two weeks, long enough for the Germans to possibly learn of the Allies' plan. Eisenhower gave the order and set in motion the largest amphibious invasion in world history: an armada of more than 4,000 warships, nearly 10,000 aircraft, and about 160,000 invasion troops. The hard-fought invasion was a success, although casualties were heavy in some of the beach landing areas and in the airborne drop zones inland. Eisenhower had won his gamble with the weather. In less than two months, Allied forces broke out from their Normandy beachheads and pushed through France and on to Germany, resulting in the eventual collapse and surrender of Nazi Germany and the liberation of Europe.

What was especially noteworthy about Eisenhower's actions and demeanor in those final days before the invasion? I am using his story as an excellent example of commander's calm, a label I use to describe the behavior and demeanor of leaders who demonstrate exceptional calm, poise, and composure under extreme conditions. General Eisenhower kept his wits about him while surrounded by strong disagreements among his staff; generals with strong egos; planning challenges of the largest armada ever assembled with multiservice, multinational components; and, of course, the great uncertainty of the weather. Through all this, he was a calm and confident leader, very much informed and very much in control.

In reading about and personally observing commanders of military fighting units, it strikes me how the best leaders always appear so calm and composed in combat, while the poor ones always seem to be in a tizzy. On a personal note, I had to quickly learn how to be more like an Eisenhower to successfully lead a company of men in combat.

While I was serving as an officer in the war in Vietnam, there were many times when my company came under fire. It was a hard-fought war, and we were on the front lines. I always kept in the forefront of my mind what I had learned from my first sergeant: A true leader does not just dictate what others should do, but leads by his own actions. One night, my men and I were moving through the jungle when we were ambushed by the enemy. Gunfire seemed to come from all around. I positioned my men to where we were able to hold off the attack, but then realized the enemy's point element was working to establish crossfire over our unit. While the men of my company held off the enemy as much as possible, I was able to crawl to the enemy's emplacement and destroy it with a hand grenade. Then we were able to move forward with an assault that got us out of that dangerous battle. I was later awarded the Silver Star for this action. While I am very proud of the honor bestowed on me, this was just one instance of many during Vietnam where my training and ability to focus on the moment allowed me to take the actions that were needed to achieve success.

My combat experience is one of the factors that led me to want to study leadership and leader development and, eventually, human performance in a broader sense, especially performance under extreme conditions. My own experiences throughout my career continued to develop my interest and passion for the field of sports and performance psychology, eventually bringing me to where I am now.

The ability to remain cool, calm, and collected under fire is critical to performing well in any situation, but absolutely essential in a VUCA environment.

Commander's calm is the capacity to respond mentally, emotionally, and physiologically in a calm and composed manner, regardless of the tempo, clarity, or comfort level of the situation. Interestingly enough, in *Merriam-Webster's Dictionary*, one definition of *calm* is "a period or condition of freedom from storms, high winds, or rough activity of water." The same could be said for human calm. It is not so much the presence of a certain state, for example, being relaxed or steady, but the *absence* of a certain state, for example, stress, worry, or anxiety. Of course, the absence of a certain state is most effectively derived by the presence of a different state. You cannot be stress- or worry-free without applying something you have specifically learned through experience or deliberate training.

Mental skills play a crucial role in the development of the leader capacity for *commander's calm*. As I mentioned earlier, it is not what happens to you that really matters; it is how you *think* about what happens to you that matters. We act on what we perceive and how we interpret the world around us. The interpretation is totally within our control, if we choose to exercise it. We have the opportunity, through our thoughts, to choose whether a situation is perceived as threatening or comforting, good or evil, helpful or hurting. And most important, that choice determines how our mind and body responds mentally, emotionally, and physiologically.

Learning to exercise voluntary control over otherwise involuntary mechanisms goes a long way in achieving the sense of calm and composure that is a distinguishing feature of successful leaders who excel in extreme conditions. I learned quickly in my early days of commanding an infantry company in Vietnam that one of my primary responsibilities was to maintain a calm and collected disposition and ensure that my men sensed it. Had I known then what I know now, that disposition would have been much easier to achieve and would have come a lot faster. Of course, experience teaches many of us about the capabilities that mental skills training provides, but specific, targeted training accelerates the learning, acquisition, and application of these mental skills.

GET COMFORTABLE WITH BEING UNCOMFORTABLE

One final point: One of the groups we have worked with is the Special Operations Command of the army. They need to be exceptionally effective under extreme conditions. Nothing less is acceptable. In a VUCA environment, warriors need to be at their best on a personal level, significantly adding to their technical, tactical, and physical proficiency. They must possess certain *capacities* that are significantly enhanced by mental skills that have been demonstrated to be critical for exceptional performance in extreme conditions. They need to have capacities that most effectively respond to challenges from rapidly evolving, ever-changing, ambiguous situations by providing a sense of control. In the VUCA battlefield, the most critical are situational awareness, mental agility, learned instinct, and commander's calm. This applies to everyone living in a VUCA world, including business executives.

In Special Operations scenarios, the windows of opportunity open and close quickly. Warriors need to prepare themselves ahead of time by developing mental skills that provide them with the tools for recognizing, understanding, and acting on those windows of opportunity. Certainly using the mind to envision a future is right at the top of such skills. The ability to create a clear image of the desired end state and then articulate that vision to others is critical for unit alignment.

The best way to communicate that vision to others is through storytelling. If the right story is told at the right time in the right way, others will see the same "picture." Fewer words, less paper, and no PowerPoints! In addition, sensing a situation accurately calls for fine-tuning all our senses, and then trusting them to provide the needed clarity for simplifying complex situations. The ability to be adaptive and agile, to be *comfortable being uncomfortable*, is fundamental for timely and effective action. The VUCA world places an absolute premium on the mental skills that develop confidence, awareness, adaptability, agility, and resilience.

EPILOGUE

I F YOU WANT TO be extraordinary, you must train extraordinarily! Doing what you have always done leads to the same old results. If you want different results in your life, and if you want to succeed, you need to make changes to make it happen. In the VUCA battlefield, Special Ops warriors must always look for new and different ways to do things, to keep the enemy from learning their patterns. They must attain and sustain exceptionally high levels of confidence, self-control, and self-regulation. They must train themselves to be self-aware leaders who can keep their eyes on the prize; maintain a positive, optimistic, and adaptive mindset; have razor-sharp focus amid distractions; and remain cool, calm, and composed under fire. In a world of uncertainty and ambiguity, we cannot "train to the test."

These skills are no longer necessary only for elite military. As I have shown, we are all living in a VUCA world. We all have to be ready for constant change and upheaval. Therefore, we all need to master the mental skills necessary not only for survival but for success in this new environment.

This differs from just developing competencies and abilities. Mental skills education and training add *root skills* that significantly enhance their application to performance. In critical situations, one action changes everything, and the leader must be prepared to be the one to make it. What good is experience if a person does not reflect on it through the lens of awareness, self-reflection, self-control, and self-regulation?

Now that you understand the VUCA environment that we live in today, and the capacities needed to become a peak performer in these situations, keep practicing your skills to train your own brain for success.

ACKNOWLEDGEMENTS

I am humbled and grateful to have had so many people contribute to my life and work over the years. This book can't contain all the gratitude I feel, but I hope to name a few and beg forgiveness of those whose names I failed to mention here.

Thanks to the people at West Point who helped inspire the Performance Enhancement Center and those who continue the legacy today of peak performance. Coach Jim Young, Coach Bob Sutton, Bruce Batten, Ned Doyle, Bill Francis, Robert Brown, Carl Ohlson, and many more. . . .

I want to thank Brian Hackett, my partner, for pushing all those years to start the business and follow my passion of helping others.

Thank you to Stephen S. Power at AMACOM, along with Betsy Thorpe and Karen Alley.

Thanks to the Jedi Masters at Apex Performance: Lisa Grossman, Amy Toms, Marcus Washington, and James Schwabach, for all their help and support, and for letting Yoda help lead the way.

Thank you also to Christa Csoka and Susan Wolfe, for their efforts to keep it all together.

NOTES

CHAPTER 3

1. *A Leader Development Strategy for a 21st Century Army* (Washington, DC: U.S. Army, 2009).

2. Thomas H. Davenport and John C. Beck, *The Attention Economy: Understanding the New Currency of Business*, rev. ed. (Watertown, MA: Harvard Business Review Press, 2002).

3. Ibid., p. 7.

CHAPTER 4

1. Henriette Anne Klauser, *Write It Down, Make it Happen: Knowing What You Want— and Getting It!* (New York: Simon & Schuster, 2001).

2. *Touching the Void*, DVD, directed by Kevin Macdonald (S GOLD Deluxe Video Services, 2003).

3. Joe Simpson, *Touching the Void: The True Story of One Man's Miraculous Survival* (New York: HarperCollins, 2004).

CHAPTER 5

1. *The Reader's Digest* 51 (September 1947): 64.

CHAPTER 6

1. Richard S. Lazarus and Raymond Launier, "Stress-Related Transactions Between Person and Environment," *Perspectives in Interactional Psychology* (1978): 287-327.

2. T.H. Holmes and R.H. Rahe, "The Social Readjustment Rating Scale," *Journal of Psychosomatic Research* 11 (1967): 213-221.

3. Ibid.

4. American Institute of Stress, "Workplace Stress," www.stress.org/workplace-stress/.

5. Ibid.

6. "Understanding the Stress Response," www.health.harvard.edu, March 1, 2011 (accessed December 21, 2015).

7. Sonia J. Lupien, Bruce S. McEwen, Megan R. Gunnar, and Christine Heim, "Effects of Stress Throughout the Lifespan on the Brain, Behaviour and Cognition," *Nature Reviews Neuroscience* 10 (June 2009): 434-445.

8. Navy SEAL + SWCC Scout Team, Naval Special Warfare Command, "Navy SEAL Frequently Asked Questions," www.sealswcc.com (accessed December 21, 2015).

9. Robert M. Yerkes and John D. Dodson, "The Relation of Strength of Stimulus to Rapidity of Habit-Formation," *Journal of Comparative Neurology and Psychology* 18 (1908): 459-482.

10. Hans Selye, "A Syndrome Produced by Diverse Nocuous Agents," Nature 138 (1936): 32.

11. Herbert Benson with Miriam Klipper, *The Relaxation Response*, reissue ed. (New York: HarperTorch, 2000).

12. Edmund Jacobson, *Progressive Relaxation*, 2nd ed. (Chicago: University of Chicago Press, 1938).

13. Edmund Jacobson, "Variation of Blood Pressure with Skeletal Muscle Tension and Relaxation," *Annals of Internal Medicine* 12 (1939): 1194-1212.

14. Wolfgang Luthe, *Autogenic Training* (New York: Grune & Stratton, 1965).

15. Richard H. Harvey, Marla K. Beauchamp, Marc Saab, and Pierre Beauchamp, "Biofeedback Reaction-Time Training: Toward Olympic Gold," *Biofeedback* 39 (2011): 7-14.

16. James B. Stewart, "Looking for a Lesson in Google's Perks," *New York Times*, March 15, 2013.

17. Darren E.R. Warburton, Crystal Whitney Nicol, and Shannon S.D. Bredin, "Health Benefits of Physical Activity: The Evidence," *Canadian Medical Association Journal* 174(2996): 801-809.

CHAPTER 8

1. Christopher Clarey, "Olympians Use Imagery as Mental Training." *New York Times*, February 22, 2014.

2. Billy Cundiff, interview, Apex Performance, 2014. www.apexperform.com/billy-cundiff.

3. *Blue Angels: A Year in the Life*, DVD, directed by Brian J. Kelly (Henninger Productions, 2005).

4. University of Maryland Center for Integrative Medicine, www.compmed.umm.edu (accessed December 21, 2015).

5. Carolyn Gregoire, "The Brain-Training Secrets of Olympic Athletes," *Huffington Post*, February 11, 2014.

CHAPTER 10

1. H.R. McMaster, *Learning from Contemporary Conflicts to Prepare for Future War* (Foreign Policy Research Institute, October 2008).

2. Peter Vaill, *Learning as a Way of Being: Strategies for Survival in a World of Permanent White Water* (San Francisco: Jossey-Bass, 1996).

3. IBM 2010 Global CEO Study, press release, May 18, 2010.

4. Partial transcript, Denver Air Route Traffic Control Center: Federal Aviation Administration, i2.cdn.turner.com/cnn/2009/images/11/27/nw.transcripts.faa.pdf.

5. Edmund Rolls, *Memory, Attention, and Decision-Making: A Unifying Computational Neuroscience Approach* (Oxford: Oxford University Press, 2007).

6. "Boeing's CH-47 Chinook Helicopter—Waging the War Against Terrorism," Chinook-helicopter.com (accessed December 21, 2015).

7. "Think This Is Real?" www.hummerxclub.com/forum/viewtopic. php?t=1078&p=20278, September 15, 2006 (accessed Dec 21, 2015).

8. "FAA Releases Transcript from Hudson River Landing," abcnews.go.com/Travel/story?id=6802512&page=1 (accessed December 21, 2015).

9. "New York Plane Crash: Pilot Chesley Sullenberger Describes 'Surreal' Landing," www.telegraph.co.uk (accessed December 21, 2015).

10. Matt Phillips, "Pilot Chesley 'Sully' Sullenberger: What Role Did Glider Flying Play?" blogs.wsj.com, January 16, 2009 (accessed December 21, 2015).

11. "General Dwight D. Eisenhower Launches Operation Overlord," www.history.com (accessed December 21, 2015).

INDEX